WOMEN, POWER AND POLITICS

NOW

ACTING LEADER
Joy Wilkinson

THE PANEL
Zinnie Harris

PLAYING THE GAME
Bola Agbaje

PINK
Sam Holcroft

YOU, ME AND Wii
Sue Townsend

Also available in a companion volume:

THEN

THE MILLINER AND THE WEAVER by Marie Jones
THE LIONESS by Rebecca Lenkiewicz
HANDBAGGED by Moira Buffini
BLOODY WIMMIN by Lucy Kirkwood

WOMEN, POWER AND POLITICS
NOW

JOY WILKINSON ▪ ACTING LEADER

ZINNIE HARRIS ▪ THE PANEL

BOLA AGBAJE ▪ PLAYING THE GAME

SAM HOLCROFT ▪ PINK

SUE TOWNSEND ▪ YOU, ME AND Wii

Introduced by Indhu Rubasingham

NICK HERN BOOKS
London
www.nickhernbooks.co.uk

A Nick Hern Book

Women, Power and Politics: Now first published in Great Britain in 2010 as a paperback original by Nick Hern Books Limited, 14 Larden Road, London W3 7ST, in association with the Tricycle Theatre, London

Cover designed by Ned Hoste, 2H
Cover image by feastcreative.com

Typeset by Nick Hern Books, London
Printed and bound in Great Britain by by CLE Print Ltd, St Ives, Cambs PE27 3LE

A CIP catalogue record for this book is available from the British Library

ISBN 978 1 84842 117 2

Contents

Introduction
Indhu Rubasingham

Women, Power and Politics is a season of nine exciting new
plays presented in two parts, *Then* and *Now*. Creating it has
been an important journey where theatre is reflecting, amongst
other things, the immediate politics of today. This journey
started a year ago.

In May 2009 the Tricycle had just opened *The Great Game:
Afghanistan*. I co-directed it with Nick Kent, who produced the
project at the Tricycle in North London, where he is the Artistic
Director. It was a day-long event featuring a series of twelve
new plays looking at Afghan history from the first Anglo-
Afghan War up to the present day. It was proving to be a huge
success and a very special production. Two days after the press
'day', whilst I was lying in a darkened room recovering from
this enormous endeavour, Nick called me to say that he had a
great idea he wanted to discuss. I was amazed by his
unstoppable energy. He had just read an article in *The Times*
where there was a picture of David Cameron presiding over the
then Shadow Cabinet, which consisted entirely of (white) men.
The article was discussing where the women were in the Tory
Party. Inspired by this, Nick offered me the opportunity to direct
and produce a project looking at and titled *Women, Power and
Politics* on a similar template to *The Great Game*.

It was a unique opportunity to conceive and produce a project on this scale. Where do you start? To begin with I thought
about international politics, working with writers from all over
the world. However, as I started to research, I soon realised that
given it was such a broad subject, if I went too wide I would
only be able to skim the surface. I was going to have to narrow
it down – and soon. But the statistics internationally were fasci-
nating and the issues complex. How do you define politics and
power? The canvas felt very, very big and, at times, daunting. It
is, moreover, a subject which raises such passion in people.

Opinions, both varied and extreme, were offered on what material the plays should contain. Unlike *The Great Game*, where the majority of people in this country were fairly unaware of the situation in Afghanistan, everyone is aware of this subject and holds a fervent opinion on it: whether it is Margaret Thatcher or the expenses scandal surrounding Jacqui Smith and her husband. It was also interesting how different generations had very different perspectives and agendas.

The fog slowly lifted and, after much discussion with my team (more about them soon), I decided that the theatre was going to be specific to women, power and politics in Great Britain; while the Tricycle's cinema would look at women in politics internationally; and its gallery would offer a celebration of women in Great Britain. It was also important to me that the programme would create debate and discussion amongst the audience and be of the highest artistic quality. Theatre is a fantastic medium for emotional engagement, and it is something we experience as a collective; I wanted the event to demonstrate the complexity of issues that should concern and engage everybody. In the theatre, we are not there to define answers but to provoke questions.

At the time of writing, we have just had a General Election. Women make up 22% of Parliament. There are only four women in the new Cabinet which works out at less than 20% and far less than most other Western democracies. Spain, Germany, France, Sweden, Norway, Italy, Greece, the USA and Belgium are just a few of the countries that have a much higher percentage of women in Government and in the Cabinet. Yet women make up 52% of the population of the UK. During the election campaign of 2010, it was the wives of the party leaders who had far more media coverage than any female politician or candidate. This new era of British politics is especially worrying as there seems to be little or no interest or concern about the lack of representation. This is ironic considering the fanfare surrounding 'Blair's Babes' in 1997. Why is this happening and what are the obstacles that are preventing women from entering or gaining power within the political system in this country? Is it the structure of government? The media? Society? Or is it women themselves?

I created a small team who would meet regularly to bounce ideas and discuss the project. This included Zoe Ingenhaag, Ruth Needham, Holly Conneely and Rachel Taylor. This team sometimes expanded to engage more voices, but on the whole this was the core group. Different generations of women discussing and tussling over this material was thrilling and thought-provoking. One example will serve for many: it became apparent that the two younger ones had never heard of Greenham Common and were unaware of such an enormous political event in the 1980s. This was suprising and led us to asking: why had this event been lost to a younger generation, and what is its legacy?

There were going to be two parts to this project, each containing four or five plays. The two parts would be played alternately on weekday evenings, and together on Saturdays. The first part would look at historical issues and the second part would look at the current situation. This was primarily decided in order to give the two parts a distinctive quality. Nick Kent suggested introducing a verbatim element, for which the Tricycle is renowned, and introduced me to Gillian Slovo. We met and decided that she would interview a variety of politicians and then edit the pieces to form a backbone to the whole event. They would be interspersed between the plays and give us the current reality of women politicians.

After the groundwork had been done, I started to approach playwrights, some I knew and others I did not. I went to Belfast and met Marie Jones; persuaded Zinnie Harris who was pregnant and already overly busy; commissioned old colleagues and friends with whom I hadn't worked but long admired: Moira Buffini and Rebecca Lenkiewicz, and young writers whose energy, skill and voice really impressed and excited me like Lucy Kirkwood, Sam Holcroft and Joy Wilkinson. I had just worked with Bola Agbaje on her play, *Detaining Justice*, and really wanted her perspective and zest; when Sue Townsend was interested, well, what can I say: I grew up on her writing.

I met and talked with each writer about the entire concept. Most of them chose subjects and topics that they were interested in, others I suggested ideas to, but all these playwrights were enthusiastic and passionate about the subject.

I made sure that the content of the plays did not overlap and waited impatiently for the first drafts. The National Theatre Studio very kindly hosted the project for a week in order to develop the scripts with actors. This proved invaluable for the development process.

The plays are incredibly exciting. The content, form and voice are unique in each play, and yet each packs a punch and is complex in its ideas. Viewing them alongside each other in production is bound to produce a stimulating and intense evening. It is an honour to be working with so much talent and I am grateful to the playwrights for their wonderful plays.

I have to thank Mel Kenyon for her advice and support, as well as Jack Bradley. Purni Morell and the National Theatre Studio have been very generous. It is a privilege to be working with Rosa Maggiora and Amy Hodge on this production with an incredibly talented and brilliant company of actors. None of this would have happened without my core team, and Zoe Ingenhaag has been the rock of this project. Finally, none of this would even be taking place if it were not for Nick Kent and his team at the Tricycle.

May 2010

Now was first performed at the Tricycle Theatre, London, as part of the *Women, Power and Politics* season on 8 June 2010, with the following casts:

ACTING LEADER

MARGARET BECKETT	Niamh Cusack
WOMAN	Lara Rossi

THE PANEL

CHRIS	Oliver Chris
MAURICE	Tom Mannion
BILL	Felix Scott
JASON	John Hollingworth
DAVID	Simon Chandler

PLAYING THE GAME

AKOUSA	Amy Loughton
JENNY	Lara Rossi
CHARLENE	Claire Cox

PINK

KIM	Heather Craney
AMY	Amy Loughton
BODYGUARD	Tom Mannion
BRIDGET	Stella Gonet

YOU, ME AND WII

VINCENT	Felix Scott
SHEILA	Kika Markham
KERRY	Heather Craney
COURTNEY	Amy Loughton
SELINA	Claire Cox
MARK	John Hollingworth

Director	Indhu Rubasingham
Designer	Rosa Maggiora
Lighting Designer	Matt Eagland
Sound Designer	Tom Lishman
Associate Director	Amy Hodge
Associate Producer	Zoe Ingenhaag
Dramaturg	Rachel Taylor

This text went to press before the end of rehearsals and so may differ slightly from the plays as performed.

ACTING LEADER

Joy Wilkinson

Joy Wilkinson's play *Now is the Time* opened at the Tricycle in 2009 as part of *The Great Game: Afghanistan*.

Joy's other writing credits include *Fair* (Finborough Theatre and Trafalgar Studios); *Felt Effects* (Theatre 503, Verity Bargate Award-winner); and *The Aquatic Ape* (Edinburgh Festival). She has recently completed an attachment at the National Theatre Studio and is writing a new play for the Liverpool Everyman and Playhouse. She also writes for radio and was a graduate of the BBC's inaugural Writers' Academy.

Characters

MARGARET BECKETT
WOMAN, *plays all other parts*
  LEO BECKETT
  JOHN HUMPHRYS
  CLARE SHORT
  TONY BLAIR
  PETER MANDELSON
  EXTRAORDINARY GIRL

With acknowledgements and thanks to Peter Morgan.

MARGARET. There are few people the announcement of whose death would bring tears to the eyes of everyone who knew them; John Smith was such a man. He was, as the Prime Minister said, a man of formidable intellect, of the highest ethics and of staunch integrity.

He said to me recently, 'Why would anyone bother to go into politics, unless it was to speak up for people who cannot speak up for themselves?' That feeling for others, along with his hatred of injustice, was the force which drove him – the service to which he gave his life.

Last night, he spoke at a gala dinner in London. He was in fine fettle and in high spirits. He spoke not from a text but from notes, and when he sat down I congratulated him especially on his final sentence – spoken, as it was, off-the-cuff and from the heart. They were almost the last words I heard him say. He looked at the assembled gathering, and he said: 'The opportunity to serve our country – that is all we ask.' Let that be his epitaph.

The WOMAN *hurtles on, pulling two wheelie suitcases behind her. She stops, waits, impatient. She opens one of the suitcases and gets out a box of tissues. She gives a tissue to* MARGARET.

Thank you.

MARGARET *dries her eyes.*

WOMAN. Come on.

MARGARET. I know, sorry.

MARGARET *blows her nose.*

WOMAN. May 12th, 1994. A Bailey Pageant Champagne caravan outside the house of Margaret and Leo Beckett.

MARGARET (*looks around, confused*). Leo?

WOMAN. A Bailey Pageant Champagne caravan.

The WOMAN *hands* MARGARET *the other suitcase.*
MARGARET *opens it, takes out a duvet and a duvet cover.*
The WOMAN *becomes* LEO.

LEO. Margaret? What're you doing out here?

MARGARET. I wanted to get things ready, for when we go away.

LEO. Let me do that.

MARGARET. I can manage.

MARGARET *busies herself, trying to put the duvet cover on*
the duvet.

LEO. You did well, love, from what I could tell. Got a bit
emotional myself.

MARGARET. Interns in the corridors. Old men in the dining
rooms. Everyone weeping. Almost everyone.

LEO. It takes a bit for the loss to really hit some people.

MARGARET. Lord Healey went on the radio. Blair and
Prescott are the dream ticket.

LEO. You don't want to take any notice of that.

MARGARET. You don't think it's true?

LEO. I think they should wait and see what my girl can do. We
mightn't be able to go away after all.

MARGARET. I'm not giving up our holiday.

LEO. You'll have your hands full being leader till October, at
least. And at most, who knows?

MARGARET. I can't win, Leo.

LEO. You're making a right mess of that. (*The duvet, he takes it*
off her and helps.) Mind must be on something else.

MARGARET. I just want to get on with the job.

LEO. The job isn't keeping the seat warm for what's-his-name.

MARGARET. I know, but I can't [win] –

LEO. 'Why would anyone bother to go into politics, unless it was to speak up for people who cannot speak up for themselves?' That's the job. The dream. Whatever happens, you can't lose that.

MARGARET. I need to think.

The WOMAN *grabs a nicotine inhaler from her suitcase. She sucks on it, as* CLARE SHORT.

CLARE. For fuck's sake!

MARGARET. Clare?

CLARE (*aside*). Short. (*Sucks*.) At Millbank. (*Sucks*.) Mid-May. (*Sucks, end of aside*.) That Blair's a wanker.

MARGARET. We've got to focus on the elections now.

CLARE. The elections will mean sod all at this rate. That wanker's got it all stitched up. It's a good job I've kicked the ciggies because right now – (*Sucks*.)

MARGARET. The European elections, Clare? June the 9th?

CLARE. Fuck Europe.

MARGARET. I wish I could, but as I happen to be Acting Leader.

CLARE. Repeat after me. 'I am not Acting Leader. I am actually Leader.' Check the constitution if you don't believe me.

MARGARET. I need to speak to the National Executive.

CLARE. They'll tell you the same thing. They all think you're doing a cracking job. So do the women and a fair bit of the Left, but we need to show everyone else. Get them questioning his inexperience, wondering what he actually stands for. We've got four months to turn this around.

MARGARET. I'm going to tell the NEC to bring the leadership elections forward, to July.

CLARE. You what? Why the fuck would you [do that] –

MARGARET. Lots of reasons. Mainly 1992.

CLARE. That'll never happen again.

MARGARET. You see how far John's brought us on?

CLARE. You and John.

MARGARET. We can't risk losing that momentum, getting caught up with Party issues.

CLARE. This isn't just a Party issue, Margaret.

MARGARET. If we start questioning ourselves, imagine what the rest of the house will do, the press.

CLARE. Fuck the press. We're picking the next Prime Minister.

MARGARET. As long as it's a Labour Prime Minister.

CLARE. A proper Labour Prime Minister.

MARGARET. I know, but Tony's going to win. He's very good, maybe we should just –

CLARE. Who turned this party around?

MARGARET. John. (*Pause.*) And me.

CLARE. Out of all those up for it, who's had the most leadership experience?

MARGARET. Me.

CLARE. Who's the Leader – the actual Leader – of the Parliamentary Labour Party?

MARGARET. Me.

CLARE. Honestly now, think about it and tell me, who is the best person for the job?

Pause. MARGARET *smiles.*

Can't hear you, Margie? Who's the best?

MARGARET. Me.

CLARE. Who's the best?

MARGARET. Me. Me. Me.

CLARE. So who's going to win?

Pause.

MARGARET. We are.

CLARE. If we don't believe it can happen, how can we expect anyone else to?

MARGARET. I believe it will happen. In July.

CLARE. No.

MARGARET. *I'm* Leader, actually. And I say we've got to get this out of the way so the Party can get back to full strength. We can't afford to lose. Not again. (*Pause.*) We can do it, can't we?

CLARE. We'll win the leadership, Europe and the fucking World Cup. Come on!

CLARE *puts down her inhaler and passes* MARGARET *some pencils.* MARGARET *wraps an elastic band around them to make a bundle as the* WOMAN *grabs a microphone.*

WOMAN. 30th May. A Gallup Poll for the BBC's *On the Record* with John Humphrys.

The WOMAN *becomes* JOHN HUMPHRYS.

HUMPHRYS. 'Who do Labour Party members think should be the next leader'?'

MARGARET. The results –

HUMPHRYS. The results are:

MARGARET. Tony –

HUMPHRYS. Tony Blair – forty-seven per cent.

MARGARET. John –

HUMPHRYS. John Prescott – fifteen per cent.

MARGARET. John, if you'll please let me –

HUMPHRYS. Gordon Brown – eleven per cent.

MARGARET. – let me finish.

HUMPHRYS. Margaret Beckett...

He points the mike at her. Waits.

Margaret Beckett...?

MARGARET. Five per cent. (*Quickly adding.*) Robin Cook –

He takes the mike back.

HUMPHRYS. Robin Cook – three per cent. Don't Know – nineteen per cent.

MARGARET *grips her bundle of pencils, galvanised.*

MARGARET. Nineteen per cent. That's where we start. When the contest starts. Which isn't yet.

WOMAN. The next day, Blair and Brown meet up at Granita Restaurant, Islington. In the absence of primary evidence, we have to rely on Peter Morgan's excellent television drama, *The Deal.* (*To* MARGARET, *handing her a can of McEwan's.*) Can you?

MARGARET. I can try.

They recreate the Granita scene, with MARGARET *playing* BROWN *and* WOMAN *playing* BLAIR. BLAIR *has a champagne glass.* BROWN *cracks the can open and swigs.*

BLAIR. Now, look. All I want, all I have ever wanted, is to get out of opposition and become part of a Labour Government. If I thought that having you as Leader would give us the best chance of achieving that, believe me, I'd step aside in a second.

BROWN. Bollocks.

BLAIR. That is the truth.

BROWN. A man who does what you have done in the last few days, that's not a man who stands aside.

BLAIR. We all come into politics for the big job.

Beat.

MARGARET. I've got the big job, at this point. But I'm not in *The Deal*.

WOMAN. Excellent though it is.

MARGARET. There is a bit of my speech to the House of Commons.

WOMAN. In voice-over. Exposition about the death of John Smith.

MARGARET. Perhaps they couldn't find an actress to play me. They tend to be attractive, actresses.

She consoles herself with another swig. The WOMAN *takes the can back.*

WOMAN. The Labour leadership contest officially begins on June 9th, after the results of the European elections.

MARGARET. We did well. Forty-four per cent. Not that anyone really noticed.

WOMAN. Between John Smith's death and the contest beginning, Tony Blair is mentioned in four hundred and eighty-two newspaper reports about the leadership, mostly positive. Margaret Beckett is mentioned in one hundred and seventy-two, mostly negative.

MARGARET. It's not too bad, given our limited resources.

WOMAN. Blair has access to £79,000 funding. Prescott has £13,000.

MARGARET. We have two students who turned up at Millbank out of the blue. One of them saw me giving a speech on television and felt compelled to help me win. Extraordinary girl.

The WOMAN *puts on a Communist red-star cap and becomes the* EXTRAORDINARY GIRL.

GIRL. I'd seen her before, but not in charge. Suddenly there was this Leader, this woman, giving as good as she got in Parliament. PM's Questions. Everything. I knew what I had to do. I grabbed my suitcase and my boyfriend and dragged them both down to London on the next train. We campaigned for her to win, stuffed envelopes, rang MPs, tried to get them to see what I could see.

MARGARET. It wasn't easy.

WOMAN. Mid-June. Tony Blair meets up with Margaret Beckett, at a hotdog stand in St James's Park.

She becomes BLAIR, *buying a hotdog. He looks around for* MARGARET.

BLAIR. Margaret? Ah, there you are. Can I tempt you?

MARGARET. No, thank you.

BLAIR. Thought you'd be singing one of your arias. To celebrate. Europe.

MARGARET. My arias are mostly tragic.

BLAIR. Is that why you sing them at Labour Party knees-ups?

MARGARET. Did you want something in particular, Tony?

BLAIR. Lots of onions, please. (*To* MARGARET.) I must say I think you're doing a fantastic job as Acting Leader.

MARGARET. Thank you. I am actually [Leader] –

BLAIR. I think it's essential that women are properly represented at top level. (*Gets hotdog, adds ketchup.*) Have you considered running for Deputy?

MARGARET. I am running for Deputy. Have you considered [running for Deputy] –

BLAIR. It can be a thankless job, but for the right person, a safe pair of hands.

MARGARET. I am running for Deputy.

BLAIR. Wouldn't it make sense to only run for Deputy? Strategically. Realistically. (*Bites the hotdog, keeps talking.*) I mean, is the country really ready for another Prime Minister called Margaret?

MARGARET. I'd hope the country could see that I only shared her name.

BLAIR. Realistically though. Look at Robin. Not even running because, well, do people really want to look at Robin?

MARGARET. I think Robin had a lot to offer. So did Gordon.

BLAIR. Yes, but strategically –

MARGARET. Strategically you and John are the dream ticket. But what's the dream?

BLAIR. What's the… what?

MARGARET. For the Labour Party. What's the –

BLAIR. Oh. Getting elected. Obviously.

MARGARET. You have ketchup on your chin.

BLAIR. Who do you think will win – the World Cup?

MARGARET. I've always supported England.

BLAIR. We aren't in it. Didn't have a hope with Old Turnip Head in charge.

MARGARET. I've been a bit busy.

BLAIR. Some people say they're backing Ireland now. But really everybody knows, it's got to be Brazil. (*Beams*.) Fancy a kickabout?

MARGARET *shakes her head. The* WOMAN *becomes* JOHN PRESCOTT, *slurping a Cornetto*.

PRESCOTT. How about an ice cream then? (*Aside*.) John Prescott, over at the Mr Whippy van. (*As* PRESCOTT.) Sweltering. Can I get you a Cornetto?

MARGARET. No, thank you.

PRESCOTT. Bit fancy, I know, but you can't fight progress. (*Slurp*.) Have you considered only running for Leader?

MARGARET. Have you considered only running for [Leader] –

PRESCOTT. I'm in a different position though. I've just got to chuck enough… not shit. You know what I mean.

MARGARET. You mean you're scared I'll get Deputy?

PRESCOTT. I mean, it sends the wrong signal. Like you don't really think you can be Leader, which is rot. You're being it now. Look at you. Smashing.

MARGARET. I'd be glad to have you as my Deputy, John, if that's what the members decide.

PRESCOTT. I wouldn't be running for both if I were Leader. I'd be putting my foot down. You don't have to do stuff just cos the sisters are pushing you into it.

MARGARET. Sorry, because the…?

PRESCOTT. Cor, what a scorcher. (*Slurp.*)

MARGARET. I've got to get back to work.

WOMAN. Early July, in the Bailey Pageant Champagne caravan.

She opens a newspaper, as LEO.

MARGARET. Leo? What are you doing out here?

LEO *quickly hides the newspaper under the duvet.*

LEO. Who needs to go on holiday, weather like this?

MARGARET. I've seen the papers already, there's no need to hide them.

She lifts the duvet, gets the paper out.

LEO. That's the kind of searing intuition a Prime Minister needs.

MARGARET. Apparently there are more important attributes. 'Children puking on your clothes is a good way of keeping perspective.'

LEO. 'Families, politics, rock and roll.'

MARGARET. 'Blair today, Number 10 tomorrow.'

LEO. There is a question mark. 'Number 10 tomorrow?'

MARGARET. Is that where I went wrong, not getting puked on?

LEO. You haven't gone wrong.

MARGARET. One member one vote?

LEO. I don't know, love. You have to wonder.

MARGARET. What?

LEO. It was meant to be more democratic, but maybe people like being told what to do. If not by the unions, then [the newspapers]…

MARGARET. 'At university, he was a love machine. Nobody's ever said that about his leadership rivals John Prescott or Margaret Beckett.'

LEO. Well, I can't speak for Prescott…

MARGARET. Thank goodness for that.

LEO. Maybe I should give them some photos of us.

MARGARET. Have you lost your mind, Leo?

LEO. Not of that. Of this. Us, working together.

MARGARET. It's not rock'n'roll.

LEO. Oi, we've got the luxury shower suite now.

MARGARET. It's not how I do things.

LEO. Just keep doing what you're doing, girl. We'll get there.

MARGARET. How's Ireland doing? In the World Cup.

LEO. Knocked out by the Netherlands. Why?

MARGARET. It doesn't matter.

The WOMAN *becomes* CLARE, *sucking on her inhaler double-time.*

CLARE. For fuck's sake!

MARGARET. Clare, how's it going? Who have we got backing us?

CLARE. We've definitely got the Campaign Group.

MARGARET. Great. Who else?

CLARE. Gordon's sending his interns over to help us stuff envelopes.

MARGARET. What about the women? (*Pause*.) The women, Clare? We've got their vote… haven't we?

CLARE. Everyone thinks you're doing a great job, but they think he's going to win, so…

MARGARET. They have no choice.

CLARE. They have no balls.

MARGARET. It's understandable, if they don't want to end up on the backbenches.

CLARE. It's a fucking nightmare.

MARGARET. If he can do this, imagine. We'd win a general election.

CLARE. But who would we be?

MARGARET. Tony's exceptional in many ways.

CLARE. This is the Labour Party.

MARGARET. I know, but. We can't win.

CLARE. We never could bloody win. That wasn't the bloody point.

MARGARET *has been twisting the elastic band around her pencils. It snaps.*

Sorry. I shouldn't have said that.

MARGARET. No, neither should I. But as long as nobody else heard.

MARGARET *looks around, picks up her pencils.*

CLARE. What? Margaret, what are you thinking?

MARGARET. The point is we have to believe that we can win. So that he'll believe it. So he won't dare just push us aside and forget, everything. So. Who's going to win?

Pause.

CLARE. We are?

MARGARET. Who's going to win?

CLARE. We are.

MARGARET. I can't hear you, Shorty. Who's going to win?

CLARE. You are.

MARGARET *gets an envelope from the suitcase.*

MARGARET. Let's get fucking stuffing.

WOMAN. July 20th, the night before the Leadership elections. Margaret throws a small party at Westminster for her supporters. Leo, Clare, the Extraordinary Girl.

MARGARET *pops a party popper. The* WOMAN *puts on the* EXTRAORDINARY GIRL *hat.*

GIRL. I don't get why we're having the do the night before. Shouldn't we wait till we've won to get wankered?

MARGARET. We couldn't wait any longer. And I wanted to thank you for your hard work, lest it get forgotten in all the fuss of us winning.

GIRL. Bring it on!

MARGARET. Brazil might have won the World Cup.

CLARE. Wankers.

MARGARET. But when it comes down to it, I believe people will still support their own side. Whatever they may say today, they'll make the right decision tomorrow.

LEO. A toast. To England. And to Margaret Beckett, Leader of the Labour Party.

MARGARET. Thank you, Leo. Everyone. Excuse me.

WOMAN. Margaret steps into the corridor for a moment, and meets Peter Mandelson.

A tearful MARGARET *quickly pulls herself together.*

MARGARET. Oh, sorry. I didn't see you there, Peter. (*Pause.*) Peter? Are you doing it?

WOMAN. I'm not sure... I don't think I can do him. (*Tries, fails.*) Can you?

MARGARET. I wouldn't know where to begin.

WOMAN. Okay, okay. I'll just have to...

The WOMAN *takes a moment to approximate* PETER MANDELSON *and indicates for* MARGARET *to go on.*

MARGARET. Hello, Peter.

MANDELSON. Mmm.

MARGARET. Working late?

MANDELSON. Mmm.

MARGARET. Peter?

MANDELSON. Mmm?

MARGARET. Do you remember my speech, when John died? Do you remember what I said? What he said.

MANDELSON (*long pause, suspicious*). Why?

MARGARET. It doesn't matter. Good luck for tomorrow.

MANDELSON. Mmm.

MANDELSON goes. MARGARET *cries. The* WOMAN *becomes* LEO.

LEO. Margaret, love? Who are you talking to?

MARGARET. No one.

LEO. Are you alright?

MARGARET. I was just thinking about John.

LEO *gets a tissue, wipes her eyes, kisses her.*

LEO. Come on, girl. You can do it.

MARGARET *blows her nose, throws the tissue away.*

MARGARET. Let's get on with it.

WOMAN. July 21st, 1994. (*As* HUMPHRYS.) The results of the Leadership ballot are in.

She hands the mike to MARGARET.

MARGARET. Do I really have to…?

HUMPHRYS. I'm going to have to press you for an answer on this.

MARGARET. Tony Blair – fifty-seven per cent. John Prescott – twenty-four per cent. Margaret Beckett – nineteen per cent.

HUMPHRYS. And the results of the deputy leadership ballot? I'm really going to have to press you.

MARGARET. John Prescott – fifty-six point five per cent. Margaret Beckett – forty-three point five per cent.

HUMPHRYS. So the dream ticket has won and the Acting Leader Margaret Beckett doesn't even get her old job back.

MARGARET. Can I go on holiday now?

WOMAN. She goes to say goodbye to her team, in a hotel room near Russell Square.

CLARE *puts a fag in her mouth.*

CLARE. Wankers.

MARGARET *takes the fag from her.*

MARGARET. We can work with wankers, happily.

MARGARET *gets a remote control.*

Come on, let's see what's on telly.

She gets under the duvet and puts the telly on.

Tony.

She changes channels.

Tony. (*Changes.*) Tony. (*Changes.*) Tony.

CLARE *takes the remote.*

CLARE. I'll find us an old film. Before he was born.

MARGARET. I wasn't beautiful enough.

CLARE. You got forty-four per cent.

MARGARET. Forty-three-and-a-half.

CLARE. Who gives a fuck?

MARGARET. I don't know, Clare. I don't know. I think we've lost… something.

CLARE. Forty-four per cent though. And nineteen. We did enough. He'll have to give you one of the big four. With your form in Treasury, what do you reckon? First woman Chancellor?

MARGARET. At least the Tories don't have anyone like him. It won't be 1992 again.

CLARE. Never again. (*At the telly.*) Richard and Judy, look. That'll have to do.

MARGARET *sings the aria 'Un Bel Di, Vedremo' from* Madam Butterfly. *The* WOMAN *speaks.*

WOMAN. Blair offered Margaret the post of Shadow Health Secretary. Not one of the big four. But she took it, and she went on to be President of the Board of Trade, Leader of the House, Environment Secretary, Foreign Secretary, and Minister of State for Housing. In May 2010, she was re-elected to serve her final term, the longest-serving female MP still there. Still there.

Lights down on MARGARET *singing.*

The End.

THE PANEL

Zinnie Harris

Zinnie Harris is a playwright and theatre director. Her plays include *Fall* (Traverse Theatre/Royal Shakespeare Company); *Julie* (National Theatre of Scotland); *Midwinter* and *Solstice* (both Royal Shakespeare Company); *Nightingale* and *Chase* (Royal Court); *Further Than the Furthest Thing* (Royal National Theatre/Tron Theatre, winner of the Peggy Ramsay Playwriting Award and the John Whiting Award); *By Many Wounds* (Hampstead Theatre). She wrote a new version of *A Doll's House* for the Donmar Warehouse in 2009. She has also written two ninety-minute dramas for Channel 4 – *Born with Two Mothers* and *Richard is My Boyfriend,* and episodes for the BBC 1 drama series *Spooks*. She was Writer-in-Residence at the Royal Shakespeare Company from 2000 – 2001, and is currently an Associate Artist at the Traverse Theatre, Edinburgh.

Characters

CHRIS
MAURICE
BILL
JASON
DAVID

Five men behind a table. JASON, BILL, CHRIS, MAURICE *and* DAVID.

In front of them, a jug of water, and some biscuits. The table is littered with pieces of paper.

CHRIS *is the chairperson,* JASON *is the shit-hot guy from another office,* DAVID *is close to retirement and* MAURICE *and* BILL *are mid-career.* MAURICE *can be cantankerous,* BILL *pensive.*

CHRIS. the door isn't quite closed

MAURICE. I didn't like her

CHRIS. the door isn't quite shut, can we shut it first?

> *One of the men goes and shuts the door.*

> honestly, for goodness' sake

MAURICE. I hadn't heard you

CHRIS. is it shut now?

BILL. yes.

JASON. she'd gone don't worry

CHRIS. had she?

> *Beat.*

BILL. well I'll start if you want

CHRIS. okay

MAURICE. I thought she was poor actually, I was more hopeful when I saw her CV but her performance, okay the presentation was acceptable but her answers

CHRIS. poor, as strong as that?

BILL. I thought I was going to start...?

MAURICE. yes, not only did she not answer the questions

JASON. she was nervous

MAURICE. but she seemed not to really understand what we were asking

JASON. nerves are no excuse anyway in my book

BILL. is anyone interested in what I think?

MAURICE. no I'm not saying that

DAVID. I disagree, nerves okay not an excuse but

MAURICE. what are you saying? *We* should have worked to put her at her ease?

CHRIS. the questions were very clear

DAVID. well we could have done

JASON. you're supposed to be nervous that's the point

MAURICE. not so nervous you don't present yourself well

CHRIS. presentation is part of the job, will be

DAVID. we don't know her circumstances, that is all I am saying

MAURICE. I think she hadn't thought it all through properly, she hadn't –

DAVID. did we offer her a tea?

MAURICE. collected her thoughts

BILL. she was shoddy

DAVID. she had come all the way from Darlington

MAURICE. prepared it in her mind

BILL. her reference isn't good either

MAURICE. got her story straight, she hadn't

DAVID. did we offer to take her coat?

JASON. let me see

CHRIS *hands* JASON *the piece of paper.*

CHRIS. I suppose maybe if she had been here with us longer

BILL. they all got the same

CHRIS. I know but if she had had another twenty minutes

MAURICE. I was frustrated with her

DAVID. women like that, men like that they don't perform well on-the-hoof that's all

JASON. this isn't a bad reference

BILL. I didn't say it was bad

JASON. you said it wasn't good

BILL. it doesn't…

MAURICE. let me see

BILL. what's the word, glow

The reference is handed on.

JASON. I don't know what she's got in her favour really.

  We are all more or less saying the same thing

DAVID. her age

MAURICE. a little old I thought

DAVID. well yes but

BILL. this is a young woman's game

DAVID. she's experienced

JASON. I never know what people mean when they say that

MAURICE. it means elderly

DAVID. no it means

JASON. look she isn't up to it, we are all agreed.

DAVID. they have years behind them, status

JASON. can we move on Chris?

  only time is pressing –

CHRIS. yes okay.

  Gentlemen, a decision?

  He holds her CV over the bin.

DAVID. we just move on too fast in my opinion, she is two
  minutes out of the door and here we are

JASON. we don't have all day

DAVID. sometimes a little reflection

CHRIS. Jason has to get a train

DAVID. I know but

  Beat.

MAURICE. I'm on David's side, another couple of minutes
  won't hurt

  After all not everything is about Jason's train.

  Beat

CHRIS. Jason?

JASON. fine

DAVID. just to collect my thoughts.

  Pause.

  DAVID *is thinking, everyone else waiting expectantly.*

BILL. David, she wasn't strong. None of us have had a good
  word to say about her.

  I think we're all in agreement

MAURICE. it's not you that will have to work with her

BILL. actually I will

CHRIS. will you?

BILL. if this new restructuring comes into force

JASON. occasionally.

BILL. well David's only got four months left in post

MAURICE. four months can be hell if you appoint the wrong person

JASON. whoever it is will be on notice for three, the maximum is four weeks

he'll only have to work with her for four weeks.

CHRIS. David anything?

DAVID *is still thinking*.

CHRIS. Okay, I'll put her to one side.

Just here

Not in the bin but not on the table either

Is that okay by everyone?

She can sit on her own chair.

DAVID. I liked the way she looked at you when she talked, even if I agree what she said wasn't good.

She looked honest

JASON. she looked dumb

MAURICE. she was dumb

DAVID. honesty is underrated.

CHRIS. is that it, David. Any other thoughts?

DAVID. yes

that was it.

Small I know but you asked.

CHRIS. should she go in the bin or on the chair?

JASON. bin

BILL. David's call

DAVID. chair.

> For the moment.
>
> She came from Darlington we didn't give her a cup of tea
>
> Let's keep her on the chair.
>
> *The CV is put on a chair.*

JASON. maybe we should get another chair so she can put her feet up

> *Beat.*

MAURICE. what about Miss, you know

BILL. Parvinda

MAURICE. no, the other one this morning

CHRIS. I can't even pronounce her name

MAURICE. no not her before

CHRIS. oh Vince, Susan Vince

MAURICE. yes I thought she was quite something

JASON. did you?

MAURICE. spirited

BILL. I never know what people mean when they say that

MAURICE. it means she was unpredictable, had something about her

BILL. is unpredictability something that we want?

JASON. it means gorgeous

MAURICE. what?

JASON. come on

MAURICE. I didn't even notice

JASON. what does it mean then

MAURICE. something the others haven't had, something

JASON. come on, there's no shame

  what? we all thought it

BILL. I didn't actually

JASON. she was drop-dead gorgeous and she knew it

  he, his tongue was practically on the table

CHRIS. sod off

JASON. I'm just saying

MAURICE. it's not relevant

JASON. of course it's not, but it has to be said that's all

MAURICE. why

  why does it have to be said

JASON. because we all thought it

  and no one is saying it

  look I'm not meaning

CHRIS. any other thoughts on Ms Vince

  apart from her looks

BILL. what was her reference like

CHRIS. better

MAURICE. did it glow

BILL. none of them have glowed

CHRIS. that's not true, yes I would say it did actually

  you want to see?

  He passes the reference over.

BILL. anyway even without her looks I think she could be trouble

MAURICE. really

BILL. didn't anybody else get that sense
    something…

DAVID. I know what you mean

BILL. something…

MAURICE. she's very bright

BILL. yes that isn't what I am saying but

DAVID. what are her circumstances

CHRIS. she didn't say

MAURICE. we must know, what's the gossip on her

No one knows, they all shrug. All except JASON.

CHRIS. Jason

JASON. I hardly know her

MAURICE. she was seconded to your department

JASON. briefly and it was years ago
    our paths didn't cross

BILL. you shagged her

JASON. no of course not

MAURICE. definitely then

BILL. don't look like that, you shagged just about everyone else

MAURICE. so tell us

Beat.

JASON. some of the staff they

DAVID. is this actually relevant?

JASON. you asked me to say
    shall I say?

CHRIS. well now you've started

DAVID. if you say we must disregard it

CHRIS. of course

DAVID. otherwise it's not fair, we don't know as much about the others

JASON. I'm quite happy to keep silent

MAURICE. oh for God's sake spill

JASON. well there were just little ripples around her that is all

CHRIS. ripples?

JASON. I'm not saying she was a troublemaker

CHRIS. I knew it

JASON. I'm not saying that just

MAURICE. people didn't like her

JASON. she isn't easy to get on with

BILL. you see, there

CHRIS. what sort of people

JASON. the office staff

MAURICE. I find that difficult to believe

she was so charming

JASON. we might be giving her a job of course she was

MAURICE. no I don't think it was put on

BILL. she's an operator

she knows exactly what she is doing

DAVID. I don't like people like that

MAURICE. I disagree

JASON. and you know her as well do you?

MAURICE. of course I don't

of course you have the advantage, you know more about her or you say you do

JASON. are you accusing me of something

MAURICE. we all know who you want to appoint

JASON. I want to appoint the best candidate

MAURICE. but you walked in with your mind made up

JASON. that's absurd

MAURICE. I'm just putting it out there

you more or less said so to me at coffee

JASON. I didn't even sit next to you at coffee

MAURICE. you intimated

CHRIS. gentlemen can we get back –

JASON. I was excited about her, I thought she had possibilities

Is that a crime?

CHRIS. both of you, the task in hand.

Beat.

DAVID. is anyone going to ask me, I mean I know I am old and doddery and I need a little more time than anyone else but

CHRIS. did you like her?

DAVID. no.

CHRIS. there we are then.

In the bin

MAURICE. I disagree with that decision

I'm sorry, but he's got a chair for Miss Doolittle

CHRIS. Deloitre

MAURICE. can't I get a chair for Ms Vince?

CHRIS. Okay

JASON. the gorgeous Ms Vince

CHRIS. a chair

But you will have to stand up

MAURICE. it's a point of principle, you make your appointment because of the performance that you see in front of you. How they answer the questions, their presentation and of course the reference. We didn't see anything that makes me concerned, the rest is gossip.

BILL. she tried to sue her old employers

Beat.

Jason's being discreet

CHRIS. really?

BILL. isn't that right Jason?

CHRIS. do you still want a chair?

MAURICE. how do you know that?

BILL. I hear things

you wanted the gossip, someone to spill

I've spilt

CHRIS. why?

BILL. why what?

CHRIS. why was she going to sue?

JASON. I don't know if this is strictly

DAVID. they didn't let her feed her baby in the lunch hour?

BILL. don't be absurd

CHRIS. you can't say that David

DAVID. what then?

BILL. she thought she was being passed over, isn't that the story Jason?

she thought she deserved a promotion and didn't get it

JASON. I never quite knew the details

MAURICE. and she was going to sue?

BILL. yes

JASON. she threatened to

She didn't actually

MAURICE. I don't believe it

BILL. Jason must have their number, perhaps we should get them to ring us

MAURICE. there is nothing in the reference, it doesn't suggest

BILL. no doubt it was part of the settlement

A good reference

CHRIS. Jason?

JASON. look I don't know what happened but something got nasty

CHRIS. she didn't actually sue them?

JASON. she didn't actually no.

Beat.

it's not a reason not to appoint her

BILL. why don't we ring them right now? Find out the whole story, we all know them. He used to be married to one.

CHRIS. Let's put her in the bin

shall we put her in the bin?

MAURICE. I just think we might be saying no to a good candidate.

BILL. I bet Jason's got Martin Jacobs on speed dial

JASON. I didn't want to bring it up

DAVID. I think it is relevant

BILL. You didn't like her anyway

JASON. that's not the point

MAURICE. put her on the chair

Just for now

Ms Vince's CV is put on the second chair.

CHRIS. we are going to have to make some decisions, the Director wants this to be through by this afternoon

MAURICE. that's fine by me

BILL. and Jason can get his train

JASON. it's not all about my train

BILL. I didn't mean that

JASON. if you lived at the other end of the country

BILL. of course, I'm on your side

CHRIS. gentlemen please.

BILL. you always get so het up

CHRIS. shshh.

Beat.

CHRIS *picks up another CV.*

Kate Agnew

MAURICE. no

JASON. I agree

BILL. not even on a chair

CHRIS. did anyone like her?

BILL. no

CHRIS. David?

DAVID. I can't remember which one she was

BILL. that's a no then

CHRIS *drops her CV into the bin.*

CHRIS. Wendy Raecroft I think we had a memo this morning she wouldn't be available to start for six months

JASON. did we hear why?

CHRIS. no but I think that pretty much takes her out of the running as well

MAURICE. she looks after her mother

BILL. is that relevant

MAURICE. probably not

but interesting.

DAVID. I thought she was with that publicist

MAURICE. who was he?

CHRIS. if she can't start till December

MAURICE. exactly, I'm agreeing with you

CHRIS *drops her into the bin.*

CHRIS. Emma Childs

BILL. Jason's candidate

JASON. no, that was the woman who withdrew

BILL. who was that?

JASON. we saw her yesterday

CHRIS. what did you think of Emma?

JASON. I'm just trying to find –

MAURICE. I made a note here I thought she was good

BILL. yes so did I

CHRIS. go on

MAURICE. She was impressive and intelligent

BILL. she has all the right experience

MAURICE. and she is the only one that we shortlisted origi-
nally interestingly

JASON. really?

MAURICE. yes if you will look at your records

six weeks ago, when we did the first sift, hang on I've got it
here, before we were told to shortlist female candidates only,
she was the only one that we actually put down as someone
we wanted to see

I'm not saying it should influence what we do now, it's just
interesting to note

BILL. it meant we wanted to see her, not that we were going to
appoint her

MAURICE. absolutely, I am just saying

CHRIS. but if we all liked her does it matter now?

BILL. no, I am just being accurate

We were in a different part of the process

JASON. would we be able to work with her?

CHRIS. I think so

MAURICE. you won't have to

BILL. I will though. Sometimes

After the restructure

And David of course

DAVID. can I see her reference

CHRIS. sure

you can't deny it…

BILL. glows?

JASON. can I see it after

The reference is passed to DAVID

DAVID. I liked her very much I have to admit

And her presentation

CHRIS. was good I thought

DAVID. was very good

BILL. she obviously did a competent job when she was in Belfast

Her reference is full of it

Did we hear how that went at the time

JASON. I was aware of it yes

MAURICE. can I see, after you

JASON. sure

Yes, it's very solid

He passes it to MAURICE.

CHRIS. it looks positive for Emma then

MAURICE. I think she'd be excellent, the more I think about it

JASON. I did like her I have to say

MAURICE. I never thought we would agree

DAVID. I've got a note here

here beside her name

I've made a small mark with my ballpoint pen

Not a dot, something between a dot and a dash

CHRIS. oh?

DAVID. it means there was something I was supposed to remember

I can't think now and if you wait before you jump down my throat

Something about her

It wasn't necessarily an objection

BILL. do we know her circumstances, when she would be able to start

CHRIS. three months I think

BILL. and we couldn't get her sooner

CHRIS. we could try certainly

MAURICE. you know who would really like her, the Chief Exec. Just his sort of person

JASON. and she'd be good with the Board

MAURICE. well as good as anyone can be

DAVID. now when I do a mark like that, a horizontal one

BILL. I'd like to see what she could do with the marketing team

MAURICE. so would the marketing team

DAVID. it usually means

JASON. she wouldn't stay at this post for long

MAURICE. provided she stays with the company

CHRIS. we would have to put her on a package

DAVID. ah yes I remember now

BILL. has she got family?

JASON. don't know

BILL. no mention of relocation?

CHRIS. not on her application

MAURICE. we could talk to her

CHRIS. David?

DAVID. I found her a little, and I'm not saying this is a problem but

Beat.

she was a little serious.

I thought anyway, did anyone else think?

CHRIS. serious?

DAVID. yes

Just a little, a little –

JASON. is that a problem?

CHRIS. it was an interview, we didn't ask her to sing and dance

DAVID. I'm not saying we shouldn't appoint her, and it wasn't exactly that she bored me

BILL. bored you?

JASON. it's a boring job

Let's be frank about it

DAVID. did anyone else think that, I know she is excellent on paper

JASON. and in person

DAVID. and I said I liked her too, how could I not have but, and I could live with her of course I could, I am just paid for my opinion and so I am giving it.

Here, there is the mark you see a little dash. Dull.

Beat.

I'm sorry I shouldn't have said anything.

Carry on

CHRIS. anyone else, is everyone else happy

MAURICE. I think so yes

JASON. absolutely

DAVID. as I say I could live with her

BILL. I know what he means though.

Beat.

CHRIS. do you?

BILL. a little

DAVID. thank you

Beat.

CHRIS. too serious?

BILL. not too serious

a little serious

JASON. how could she have presented otherwise

CHRIS. that's a fair point

BILL. humour can be important

David was talking before about honesty and I agree, but there are also times when you need to be able to see the funny side

JASON. so she was a little humourless, it's not a crime

BILL. of course it isn't

CHRIS. what did you think about the humour thing?

MAURICE. I'm not sure

JASON. are we really having this discussion?

BILL. it's important that we talk everything through

JASON. four days we have been at this

CHRIS. just a minute

JASON. four days and the desk is littered with CVs

she's an excellent candidate, I don't know what our problem is

MAURICE. I suppose she was a little grey

JASON. do we actually want to appoint someone today

CHRIS. of course we do

MAURICE. not warm

DAVID. I wouldn't go that far

JASON. I'm just putting it out there

Because I am not sure we can even all agree on that

BILL. it's part of the process to pick through surely

JASON. if that is the only agenda then fine

BILL. what do you mean by that?

JASON. me? Nothing

Beat.

MAURICE. do you remember Anne Castles?

She was too serious, God she was serious

CHRIS. she was a battleaxe

JASON. Emma Childs is not a battleaxe

BILL. yes but once you have got them within the organisation

MAURICE. once they age

JASON. I know, we'll get Emma back in and tell her a joke.

Is that what we should do? See how hard she laughs

MAURICE. it was Anne's downfall actually

BILL. absolutely

MAURICE. she could never see the funny side

JASON. we've got to the end of the pile

There is no one else

CHRIS. that isn't a reason to appoint her

MAURICE. there are two more CVs

And the people on the chairs

JASON. we all know they're dreadful. Both of them

Emma is excellent we all agreed.

CHRIS. of course we did, don't worry Jason, it doesn't mean we don't like her

BILL. I'm with David

There was something I couldn't put my finger on

To be completely honest she seemed a bit too good to be true

Now he mentions it

A bit too perfect

Beat.

CHRIS. In this process the candidates can ask for feedback. I can't put that

BILL. okay, we'd have to invent a bit.

CHRIS. she has every experience going, she ticks all the boxes

BILL. there must be some way that we could say something

MAURICE. let me see

CHRIS. you add up the points

We would have to give her a good reason

JASON. I've got one

CHRIS. a reason

JASON. yep.

MAURICE. I thought you liked her?

JASON. we lost our nerve.

That's the reason

Or someone did

BILL. that's not fair

JASON. Come on Bill

> We've been at this for four days, we've finally found someone we all liked, someone we can't fault even

> And that in itself becomes the fault

BILL. tell me you had no qualms

JASON. I had no qualms

MAURICE. I need some air, do the windows open in here

CHRIS. maybe we should recap

JASON. There's nothing wrong with this woman apart from possibly the fact that she is better than most of the people we already have

BILL. do you think that?

JASON. yes I do

> This department is poor, everyone knows that

DAVID. now wait a minute

MAURICE. I'm afraid I think that too.

> That is my main concern if I'm honest

> She's in a way too qualified for the position

> Can you imagine when she meets Jonathan Lyons, she'll eat him for breakfast

CHRIS. is that a reason to turn her down

JASON. not a reason you can give her in her feedback, that's for sure

MAURICE. he'll be her boss, can you see it working?

DAVID. This sort of thing is important

JASON. she is the best person for the job

DAVID. I know but you can't just parachute someone in who is far above anyone else in terms of skill

CHRIS. of course you can't, but

JASON. why can't you?

CHRIS. well that is just what we are considering

DAVID. it doesn't work

JASON. how many really talented women are in this organisation?

And I don't mean stuck in an administrative capacity. How many are actually there at the right grade for their potential

CHRIS. we can't take the responsibility for that

JASON. we are exactly where the responsibility lies

Look at us now

This is where it happens

CHRIS. how the team works of course is a consideration

JASON. I'm not saying it isn't

MAURICE. if we had had a fair recruitment process it might have been different

BILL. exactly

JASON. I'm not sure about that

MAURICE. it's going to be difficult for whoever we appoint

We have to factor that in

JASON. I disagree

BILL. would you want to be appointed this way, if you were her

JASON. yes

BILL. and once you were in the job, and word got around that you only got it because of your gender

JASON. if I was good at my job it wouldn't matter

MAURICE. if you were good at your job, you'd have got the job anyway

JASON. not necessarily.

> Not if I was Emma Childs and my crime was being better than anyone else.

> Are you opening the window or not?

DAVID. what about someone like Margaret though, no one helped her, and she made it

JASON. of course she did

> I'm not saying it can't happen

DAVID. what would she say if she was sitting here?

JASON. she'd say it was a screwed system for this lot, and they have it easy

> she would be quite angry about it no doubt

BILL. Margaret does anger well that's for sure

DAVID. think how many years she was working away and what her CV looked like before she even got a sniff at a job like this

JASON. well that wasn't fair either

BILL. I know but she never stops going on about the hard time she had

DAVID. kids at home being looked after by nannies, not seeing her husband for weeks at a time

JASON. are we advocating this?

BILL. no we're just saying that was her experience

JASON. this candidate is a good candidate

DAVID. By the time Margaret was appointed she could have run the whole building let alone this floor

CHRIS. are we going to appoint today or not?

BILL. what if she mucks up?

JASON. why would she muck up

MAURICE. because the way that this company works everyone is just waiting until you muck up

BILL. And it will be harder for her

CHRIS. I think she's up to it

BILL. she's there by the way sitting in the sun

CHRIS. where?

BILL. she must have come out of the interview and bought her lunch

MAURICE. doesn't she realise we can see her from this window

DAVID. it's a labyrinthine building

JASON. Don't tell me that is another reason not to appoint her

she hasn't got a good sense of direction.

MAURICE. well has she?

JASON. what?

MAURICE. I'm joking.

JASON. I'm not laughing.

MAURICE. you're worried about your train

JASON. it's not the only thing I'm worried about

DAVID. let me see.

DAVID *goes over to the window and looks out*.

she actually looks rather radiant sitting in the sun.

Beat.

CHRIS. so gentlemen, what's it to be?

PLAYING THE GAME

Bola Agbaje

Bola Agbaje's play *Detaining Justice* opened at the Tricycle in 2009 as part of the *Not Black and White* season. Her first play, *Gone Too Far!,* was first produced Upstairs at the Royal Court Theatre in 2007 and then transferred Downstairs for a sell-out run in 2008. The play won the 2008 Olivier Award for an Outstanding Achievement in an Affiliated Theatre.

Bola was also nominated for the Evening Standard Award for Most Promising Playwright of 2008. Her writing has been presented by the Royal Court Theatre, ATC, Tiata Fahodzi, Hampstead Theatre, the Young Vic, and Talawa. Most recently, she wrote *Everything Must Go* for Soho Theatre and *Off the Endz* for the Royal Court. She is under commission to Tiata Fahodzi and Paines Plough. Bola is also developing *Gone Too Far!* into a film script with Poisson Rouge and the UK Film Council.

Characters

AKOUSA, *eighteen, plain Jane, shy and quiet*
JENNY, *twenty, beautiful, posh and perfect*
CHARLENE, *twenty, beautiful, loud and Jenny's sidekick*

*It's that time of the year to elect a new head for the Students'
Union. Jenny and Charlene have picked their candidate:
Jenny's flatmate, Akousa.*

*Dedicated to my little sister, Bisola Agbaje. Can't believe you're
heading to college this year. How time flies.*

Scene One

We are in JENNY*'s room.* AKOUSA, *a low-maintenance girl, is dressed in a tight black bodysuit with heels. She has no make-up on and her hair is tied back in a loose bun. She looks very uncomfortable.* JENNY, *on the other hand, a high-maintenance girl, doesn't have a hair out of place and her face is caked with make-up.* CHARLENE *is present and dressed the same as* JENNY. *They both have on bling-out 'Vote for Akousa' tight T-shirts.* CHARLENE *is holding a camcorder and is pointing it at* AKOUSA.

The lights go up and music on.

JENNY *begins demonstrating a sexy dance move for* AKOUSA *to follow.* AKOUSA *attempts to copy the moves but is very stiff.* JENNY *passes her a sparkly card to hold up to the camera that reads 'VOTE ME'.* AKOUSA *holds the card upside down,* JENNY *goes up to her to adjust it.*

JENNY. Shake those hips.

    She pushes AKOUSA*'s hips.*

CHARLENE. Pout those lips.

JENNY. Lean forward, you have to make love to the camera. Like this.

    She begins to seduce the camera. AKOUSA *watches* JENNY *and tries to copy her but is not as confident.*

CHARLENE. Don't forget to mime the words.

AKOUSA. Help me out. What are the words to this song?

JENNY. We can work on the words later. Come on, you should be doing this, not me.

AKOUSA. Right.

AKOUSA *attempts to copy* JENNY *and is giving it her all.*

JENNY. Sasha Fierce is in you!

AKOUSA. Sasha Fierce? Who is that?

CHARLENE. Beyoncé's alter ego!

JENNY. Search for that superhero within you… you need to have super-sexy powers.

AKOUSA. Super-sexual powers. Right. Right.

AKOUSA *stops.*

JENNY. Why you stopping for?

AKOUSA *goes and gets a notepad and pen and prepares to take notes.*

AKOUSA. What does my alter ego look like?

JENNY. You. But the fearless you.

AKOUSA *begins to write the note down.*

AKOUSA. Got to be fearless.

JENNY *takes the notepad from* AKOUSA.

I really wanna get this right.

JENNY. Stop stressing, you're getting there. Just need to get more rhythm.

AKOUSA. You don't think I have rhythm?

CHARLENE. You just need to loosen up a bit. You're way too stiff.

JENNY. And once you do, Madonna will have nothing on you.

AKOUSA. Right!

She begins to dance to the song again.

JENNY. That's it. Dance. You've got it.

CHARLENE. Shake what your mama gave ya! (*To* JENNY.) Always wanted to say that!

JENNY. Issues!

AKOUSA. How are my hips looking?

JENNY. Don't worry, you look good!

CHARLENE. You can do this.

JENNY. You look sexy!

AKOUSA. Just call me Electra!

CHARLENE. Electra?

AKOUSA. That's the name of my alter ego.

JENNY Okay, Electra, push your bum out.

AKOUSA. I am.

JENNY (*to* CHARLENE). Put bum-pads on the shopping list.

AKOUSA. My arse is fine how it is.

> JENNY *takes out some gel pads from her bra and hands them to* AKOUSA.

JENNY. Have these!

> AKOUSA *throws the gel pads on the floor.*

AKOUSA. Yuk! They feel horrid.

JENNY. Oi! They are expensive, I'll have you know.

CHARLENE. When you getting your boobs done?

JENNY. When my dad sends the cheque for 'em.

CHARLENE. Lucky!

> JENNY *picks up the pads* AKOUSA *threw on the floor and places them back inside her bra.*

AKOUSA. Can I take a break?

CHARLENE. The director is meant to…

AKOUSA.….I need a moment, just give me a minute. I need to process it all…

CHARLENE. You can't give up!

AKOUSA. I am not giving up. It's a lot to take in. All the steps and sexiness…

Pause. CHARLENE *goes over to the iPod and stops the music.*

…I want to get it right, want it to be perfect.

JENNY. It's gonna be perfect or we wouldn't have put a lot of time and effort into this campaign.

AKOUSA. You only decided yesterday that I should run for this.

CHARLENE. Since then we – (*She points to* JENNY.) have been up all night working.

JENNY *grabs* AKOUSA *and places her down on a chair and talks to her gently like a child.*

JENNY. You're doing a great job.

AKOUSA. My only worry is I don't know much about politics.

CHARLENE. That's the great thing 'bout politics, though, you don't need to.

JENNY. You have passion and good reasons for standing, remember what you said yesterday about the things that annoyed you about this uni and what you wanted to change. Equality for all, fairness…

AKOUSA. Yeah…

JENNY. …and what was the one that was most important to you?

AKOUSA. …making sure we got our damn student loans on time.

JENNY. There you go.

CHARLENE. This video will change the way people view politics. You could have easily done a video to talk about boring policies. But that's so nineties.

CHARLENE *is looking back at the videotape and the expression on her face is one of disgust.*

Ohhh.

CHARLENE *goes over to show* JENNY *the video.*

JENNY (*to* AKOUSA). Ooooooh. Wow!

AKOUSA. What? Let me see.

She goes over to look at the camera.

Oh my gosh, I look like I'm auditioning to be in a rapper's music video.

CHARLENE. A low-budget video.

JENNY *hits* CHARLENE.

Ouch!

JENNY. It's not a problem we can't fix. (*To* CHARLENE.) Can't we?

CHARLENE. I don't kn…

JENNY. We can! I got it. We were just missing a few ingredients, that's all. (*To* CHARLENE.) She needs the full works.

She pulls AKOUSA *over to a chair and sits her down.* CHARLENE *goes over to her bag and pulls out a make-up purse. She takes the make-up out and lays it down on the table.*

We are going to make you look like a superstar. Sprinkle a little glamour dust.

AKOUSA. I don't want to be made up!

JENNY. You don't have a choice. (*To* CHARLENE.) What look should we go for?

AKOUSA *tries to get out of the seat and* JENNY *pushes her back down.*

AKOUSA. You know I don't wear make-up.

JENNY. Ahh, sweetie, you got a lot to learn. You are going to be in the public eye and under a lot of scrutiny. You *have to look good.*

CHARLENE. Make-up is your friend. It has saved a lot of people's lives, and without it some people wouldn't even have a career.

JENNY. If you saw what Jordan looked like under all that make-up…

AKOUSA. I don't want you to make me look like Jordan!

JENNY. You're not going to. Calm down.

AKOUSA attempts to get up and JENNY *pushes her back down.* CHARLENE *turns the camera back on and begins filming* AKOUSA. JENNY *begins to apply make-up on* AKOUSA.

CHARLENE. You know what will work well for the campaign? A diary of Akousa. The people will love it. We can call it 'From Duckling to Swan'!

JENNY. Fantastic idea.

AKOUSA. Can you put the camera down, please. (*To* JENNY.) Leave my face alone.

JENNY. Stop being silly!

AKOUSA. I don't want any make-up.

CHARLENE. I don't know how to break it to you, babes, but…

JENNY. I do. You need it.

AKOUSA looks at JENNY, *offended.*

CHARLENE. Stop being a diva and let us experts get on with our jobs.

JENNY. Precisely. Number One Rule to success is Beauty.

AKOUSA. And where did you read that?

JENNY. It is not something you read. It's something you know. Unfortunately, ugly people find it hard to succeed. Ask Lady Sovereign.

AKOUSA. Who?

JENNY. There you go.

CHARLENE. No one likes fugly! We should think of putting in some hair extensions.

AKOUSA. I wouldn't mind a bit of length…

JENNY *shows* AKOUSA *a mirror quickly and takes it away before she gets a good look.*

JENNY. Don't tell me, you don't like what you see.

AKOUSA. Didn't see anything.

CHARLENE (*to* AKOUSA). Ready.

AKOUSA. Can I take a look, please?

CHARLENE. Guys, I got to get this camera back to the media suite soon. So come on.

JENNY. She's ready.

CHARLENE *puts the music back on but* AKOUSA *does not dance.*

AKOUSA. So do I…

JENNY *and* CHARLENE.…Dance!

AKOUSA *begins to dance.*

JENNY. This video is gonna be the number-one viewed on YouTube. Mark my words.

CHARLENE. We are going to build up a global fan base. Shake that money maker.

JENNY *shoots* CHARLENE *a look.*

(*To* JENNY.) What! I've always wanted to say that.

JENNY (*to* AKOUSA). Let your looks talk for you. (*To* CHARLENE.) Stunning?

CHARLENE. Yep. Stunning. Girls are gonna look at you and envy you and guy are gonna wanna…

JENNY. Fuck you!

CHARLENE. That's a bit much.

JENNY. Okay, wanna date you!

CHARLENE. And once we have them all hooked we can hit them with the boring stuff – policies, change, change, blah blah blah.

AKOUSA *dances and she is getting into it until she catches herself in the mirror behind her. She stops and turns to* JENNY *and* CHARLENE.

AKOUSA. I look like a prostitute!

JENNY. Don't stop now. Sex sells.

AKOUSA *picks up a face wipe and goes to wipe her face,* JENNY *stops her.*

AKOUSA. I am not trying to sell sex! Most women in politics don't look like this.

JENNY. And that's the problem and why so few of them get anywhere.

AKOUSA. Margaret Thatcher was once Prime Minister.

CHARLENE. How many centuries ago was that?

JENNY. And let's not forget she only got in cos she looked like a bloke. Do you want to look like a bloke?

AKOUSA. No.

JENNY. You can be the first woman in politics to really make a difference. Being attractive and easy on the eye will get you everywhere.

CHARLENE. Sure does.

JENNY. How would you know?

CHARLENE. Harsh!

JENNY. Believe me, women in politics would get a lot further if they made a bit of an effort. If I were Prime Minister I'd write a bill that all women need to look *hot*! I'd have a bouncer at the door of the Houses of Parliament to turn away the ugly-looking ones.

AKOUSA. I'm not running for Parliament, it's a student election.

JENNY. This is where it begins. You have a chance to be a role model and you can finally have men eating out of your hands.

AKOUSA. Appealing to men is not why I wanna go into politics.

CHARLENE. You said yesterday you wanted to be noticed.

AKOUSA. I said I wanted to be taken seriously. I want students in general to be taken seriously.

JENNY (*to* AKOUSA). If you don't like how we are running your campaign, why did you hire us!

AKOUSA. I didn't hire you...

CHARLENE. We are doing this for you. Are you not sick and tired of people not knowing who you are?

AKOUSA. Yes but...

JENNY. Look into the future. In a few weeks you are gonna be ruling this university. We... I mean you are gonna be the most powerful girl on campus. We have your best interests at heart, just trust us. You have seen all the other candidates and their video blogs.

CHARLENE. The only way you are going to be different, is by standing out.

AKOUSA. I know, I'm sorry. I'm just nervous, that's all...

JENNY. Happens to the best of us. But you can't be doubting yourself now that we have come this far.

CHARLENE. You are gonna be the Beyoncé of politics. Look how influential her music is.

JENNY. She created a word, 'bootylicious', and it's in the dictionary. Also got to remember you're not just doing this for you, you are doing this for your family.

AKOUSA. Yeah. My dad thinks university is for time-wasters, people who don't know what they want to do with their lives.

JENNY. Imagine the look on his face when you tell him you are the head of the Students' Union.

CHARLENE. You are doing this to prove your dad wrong…

JENNY. That's it… to prove your dad wrong. This is gonna make him proud. Let's get the show on the road.

CHARLENE *goes over to the iPod and turns the music on.*

CHARLENE. Time is money!

JENNY (*to* AKOUSA). You still wanna do this, right?

AKOUSA *agrees reluctantly.*

AKOUSA. Yeah. Let's get this show on the road!

CHARLENE. Ready.

AKOUSA. Yeah. I am gonna make my dad proud.

CHARLENE. Good.

CHARLENE *points the camera towards* AKOUSA.

And action.

AKOUSA *begins to dance.*

Scene Two

AKOUSA *enters excitingly into the room followed by* JENNY *and* CHARLENE, *who is writing into a diary and talking on the phone.* AKOUSA *still has on a full set of make-up and is wearing high heels that she can't balance in, but she doesn't seem to care. She is full of confidence.*

AKOUSA. What a buzz, that was amazing. I wanna do it again!

JENNY. You're a pro, was born to do this.

She kicks off the heels, picks up her laptop and sits on her bed.

CHARLENE. We are fully booked on the 12th, how about lunchtime on the 15th.

AKOUSA. 15th I have a meeting with the Dean.

CHARLENE (*to* AKOUSA). Shhhhh. (*Back on the phone.*) No, not you. 15th is fine. Save the questions for when you interview her.

> CHARLENE *hangs up.* JENNY *takes out a bottle of wine from under her bed. She hands out some glasses.* AKOUSA *takes it and puts it out for* JENNY *to pour her a glass.*

JENNY (*to* AKOUSA). This is exciting.

AKOUSA. I know. People actually know my name. They love me.

> JENNY *hands* CHARLENE *a glass.*

CHARLENE. It's brill! My phone hasn't stopped ringing all day.

> *A loud text message beeps on the phone.*

> *All three girls clink their wine glasses.*

CHARLENE. Cheers. We are on fire, baby!

JENNY. Did you see Dave's face? He didn't get asked one question. (*To* AKOUSA.) Everyone wanted to talk to you.

AKOUSA. He gave me his number.

CHARLENE. Knew he fancied you. You gonna call him?

AKOUSA. He's not really my type.

JENNY. Well, this is just the beginning, soon you will have them all lined up and…

> AKOUSA *has stopped paying attention. She is staring at the screen and her mouth drops opens and eyes well up.* JENNY *notices.*

…what's wrong?

AKOUSA. Oh my gosh, oh my gosh.

> JENNY *takes the laptop from* AKOUSA.

JENNY. No need to be melodramatic.

AKOUSA. It's… they are sayin'…

CHARLENE. What is it?

CHARLENE *takes a look at the laptop.* AKOUSA *begins to cry.*

JENNY. Look on the bright side.

AKOUSA. Bright side?

JENNY *and* CHARLENE. Yeah!

AKOUSA. Did you read what I…

JENNY. It's great news.

CHARLENE. People are really fast, they uploaded those pics quick.

AKOUSA. I don't think you guys un…

JENNY. Sweetie, stop being negative. The glass is half full not half empty.

AKOUSA *picks up the laptop and shows them her Facebook page.*

AKOUSA. *They are calling me a slag!*

JENNY It's a good thing.

AKOUSA. Oh, really!

JENNY. Yes. People know you now. They didn't before. They have an opinion on you. You're finally 'somebody'!

AKOUSA. The wrong kind of 'somebody'. Look at the comments. 'I'd give her one,' 'She looks loose.' 'Are you gonna bang doe.' How are people possibly gonna take me seriously? I knew I shouldn't have done this, I told you…

CHARLENE. Stop panicking. We can use this to our advantage.

JENNY. Thank you, Charlene. There is no such thing as bad publicity.

CHARLENE. Precisely. People pay thousands for this kind of exposure. We are getting it for free and we didn't have to hire a publicist.

AKOUSA. A slag is not the image I wanted created of me.

JENNY. It's only the first. As a politician you are gonna have many faces painted of you. Take that guy…

AKOUSA. What guy?

JENNY. The one that runs this country.

CHARLENE. Tony Blair.

AKOUSA. You mean Gordon Brown.

JENNY. What is the first thing you think of when you look at him?

AKOUSA. That he's fat.

JENNY. He's not fat.

AKOUSA. Yes he is?

JENNY. He's skinny and posh.

AKOUSA. I wouldn't say he is posh.

CHARLENE. Or skinny.

JENNY. The one I'm talking about is.

AKOUSA. It ain't Gordon Brown.

She types into the computer and shows JENNY.

JENNY. Er, not him.

AKOUSA. He's the Prime Minister.

JENNY. He is not the one I'm talking about.

AKOUSA. Who are you talking about?

CHARLENE (*to* JENNY). You're talking about David Cameron.

She shows a picture of David Cameron to JENNY.

JENNY. No… Nick something.

AKOUSA. He don't run the country.

JENNY. Ain't he gonna?

AKOUSA. No. You don't know who runs the country, the elections were only in…

JENNY. My point wasn't about… What I was saying… What was I saying?

CHARLENE *shrugs*.

I forgot what I was saying… It don't matter, look, Akousa, you are gonna have to learn to grow a thick skin. To survive in this game you have to be strong. Don't dwell on what people say or think about you. For everyone that loves you, there will be an equal amount of…

CHARLENE. …haters!

JENNY. You've alway wanted to use that word too?

CHARLENE. Why, you gonna 'hate' on me for using it?

JENNY *shakes her head*.

AKOUSA. You wouldn't be saying all of this if it was you.

JENNY. People have said worse things about me and you don't see me crying.

CHARLENE. Jenny.

JENNY *and* CHARLENE *go and huddle in a corner. They whisper, but loud enough for* AKOUSA *to hear*.

I think she might crack.

JENNY. She will be fine.

CHARLENE. You sure she can cope with this?

AKOUSA. I can hear you.

They look over and whisper quietly. CHARLENE *goes over to the bed and picks up the laptop. She heads back to the corner.*

JENNY. Right, we got it! We're gonna fix this problem.

CHARLENE. We got a really good idea.

JENNY. It's brilliant.

AKOUSA. I'm listening.

JENNY. The war's not over. We can recover from this.

AKOUSA. I said I am listening.

JENNY. People think you are too girly right now?

AKOUSA. The word they are using is '*slag*'!

CHARLENE. The word on Facebook and Twitter is that it's the women that have the real problem with you…

JENNY. …and it's cos they feel threatened by you.

CHARLENE. We should have seen it, most women dislike pretty women.

JENNY. As a beautiful woman myself, I'm somewhat of an expert on this subject. I have this exact problem every day. They think because I'm attractive that…

CHARLENE. Focus, Jenny…

JENNY. …they always think that I am after their men.

CHARLENE. Again, focus.

JENNY. All you need for your next video blog is a new look. We have to show them a new side of you. We are gonna strip you bare. Get you to be one of the lads.

CHARLENE. Dress up like them…

JENNY. Wear jogging bottoms. Now is a good time to go for that natural look you wanted. Women will see you and feel less threatened by you and then you will have their votes.

She finds an old pair of jogging bottoms. She throws them at AKOUSA. AKOUSA *looks at them and throws them back at* JENNY.

AKOUSA. Why aren't you guys running? You seem to know what the public want.

JENNY. Politics isn't for me.

CHARLENE. We'd rather be behind the scenes.

JENNY. Pulling strings.

AKOUSA. I'm not a puppet.

JENNY. Course not, sweetie.

She throws the jogging bottom back at AKOUSA.

Put this on.

Scene Three

JENNY *and* CHARLENE *are in the bedroom exercising, doing yoga.* AKOUSA *walks in. She ignores them and heads over to her bed.*

JENNY. Hey…

AKOUSA *continues to ignore* JENNY. *She looks around her bed for a book.*

I said hey!

She continues to ignore her. JENNY *stops her workout.*

CHARLENE. What are you doing? She doesn't want to talk to you, leave her.

JENNY. It's extremely rude when one… (*To* AKOUSA.) Where are your manners?

AKOUSA. I am not talking to you.

JENNY. Sweetie, you have to talk to us some time.

AKOUSA. Not if I choose otherwise.

CHARLENE. Can't blame us for…

AKOUSA. I've been labelled a lesbian!

JENNY. I'm sorry, but what is the problem?

CHARLENE. We didn't see that coming.

AKOUSA. It doesn't matter any more, I quit.

CHARLENE. You can't quit. We have come this far. You're the front-runner.

AKOUSA. I am the freak.

JENNY. You need to see the positive side.

AKOUSA. They are going around calling me a confused-slag-turned-lesbian.

JENNY. They didn't call you a lesbian, per se.

AKOUSA. A carpet muncher is a lesbian.

JENNY. Sweetie, you are tiring me out... People know your name. They can't stop talking about you. You have even become a trending topic on Twitter, how can you not see the positive...

AKOUSA. Everything they are saying about me is wrong. False!

CHARLENE. It doesn't matter.

AKOUSA. I want to be taken seriously.

JENNY. And in time you will. *This is great publicity*. You've got over two hundred friend requests on Facebook. I'm afraid rumours and gossip come with the territory. You are the Lady Gaga of politics.

AKOUSA. The other day I was the Beyoncé of politics.

CHARLENE. We are moving with the times. Just take it all in, enjoy it. Once the election process is over. You can go back to being yourself and all these rumours will disappear.

JENNY. Trust us. We are here to serve you.

CHARLENE. We won't let you down.

AKOUSA. My dad's been calling me, he doesn't like what he's seeing on Facebook…

CHARLENE. Your dad's on Facebook?

AKOUSA. Yes, and he's saying…

CHARLENE. Block him, that's what I did to my parents…

AKOUSA. I don't want to…

CHARLENE. Then limit his access…

AKOUSA. I don't wa…

JENNY. Look, Akousa, we have been pretty patient with you the last few days. Stop acting like a spoilt child. You do know this is a paid job?

CHARLENE. Treat this election process like an interview.

AKOUSA. I'm not the right person for this job.

JENNY. You don't have much of a choice. May I remind you, you owe me three months' back-payment in rent.

AKOUSA. I told you, I'm waiting for my loan to come through and then…

JENNY. You can't keep using that excuse. If I were you, I would count myself lucky that you have a friend like me, and I will continue to be understanding as long as you continue to be a candidate.

AKOUSA. Are you blackmailing me?

JENNY. Would I do that? Nothing in this world is free, my dear.

AKOUSA. Coming from a girl whose dad owns this house and never had to pay for anything in her life.

JENNY. Do you think I really want to be here. I'm waiting for the next round of auditions for *X Factor* and then I'm out of here…

CHARLENE. You auditioned already and got rejected…

JENNY. My nerves got the better of me. This time around I'd be ready and I'm gonna get to the finals and then my dad can't say I haven't done anything with my life. (*To* AKOUSA.) What's it gonna be?

Pause.

AKOUSA. What if I don't win?

JENNY. You will…

AKOUSA. But if I don't?

JENNY. You should concentrate on winning.

Pause.

AKOUSA. Fine.

She storms out. CHARLENE *goes after her but* JENNY *stops her.*

JENNY. Leave her. She'll come around.

JENNY *and* CHARLENE *go back to their workout.*

CHARLENE. I feel bad.

JENNY. What for?

CHARLENE. She doesn't want to do this.

JENNY. She has no choice. I am sick and tired of saying this time and time again. We're doing her a favour. She can't coast her way through life. People like her have to understand…

CHARLENE. It's not her fault she's broke.

JENNY. It's not mine either.

CHARLENE. You got to feel a little bit sorry for her.

JENNY. What for?

CHARLENE. Imagine if your parents were poor like hers.

JENNY. Never happen.

CHARLENE. Just imagine it, though. It must be really tough for her.

JENNY. That's why she should be grateful. If she wins, it's gonna open loads of doors and opportunity for her...

CHARLENE. And most importantly, us!

CHARLENE high-fives JENNY.

I can't wait. We are gonna have the whole uni eating out of our hands.

JENNY. I know. Can't wait to get my hands on the budget.

JENNY goes over to the mirror and begins to examine herself, concentrating on her breasts.

CHARLENE. We can throw the biggest party this university has ever seen.

JENNY. Get some artist to perform like Tinchy Stryder or Dizzee Rascal.

CHARLENE. We're gonna be legends.

JENNY. What we need to do is...

CHARLENE begins to daydream. JENNY notices.

You thinking what I'm thinking?

CHARLENE. If Dizzee Rascal will be up for a threesome.

JENNY. Threesome?

CHARLENE. What?

JENNY. You have issues.

CHARLENE. I was kidding.

JENNY. If you say so.

JENNY gets a paper and pen and begins to plan the party.

CHARLENE. This party will definitely get me my First.

JENNY. What?

CHARLENE. I need to get a good grade.

JENNY. Doesn't matter what grades you get. My sister told me you could put anything on your CV and employers don't check. Ask anyone who has graduated if they have *ever* needed to provide any documentation. Employers look for experience and running this campaign is the only experience you need if you are gonna be coordinating events at London Fashion Week. Just got to make sure that Akousa don't mess it up.

Pause.

CHARLENE. What are we gonna do about this lesbian thing?

JENNY. Create an even bigger and better rumour.

CHARLENE. I don't know… anything else may just push her completely over the edge.

JENNY. You got a better idea?

CHARLENE *looks at the laptop.*

CHARLENE. People on Twitter are saying they don't think she is relatable.

JENNY. What does that mean?

CHARLENE. Dunno, she's not relatable.

JENNY *takes the laptop.*

JENNY. Gosh! Those stupid geeks from the canteen. Can't they just get a life? Come.

CHARLENE. Where are we going?

JENNY. To start work on this damn manifesto they want.

CHARLENE. You forget we don't know much about politics.

JENNY. There is nothing to it. All we got to do is promise loads of changes the people want and once we got the job it won't matter. We won't have to do any of it.

Scene Four

AKOUSA, JENNY *and* CHARLENE *come into the room. They are excited and singing.* JENNY *goes over to her bed and picks up a bottle of wine. She hands the glasses to* CHARLENE *and* AKOUSA. *She pours them all a drink.* AKOUSA *goes over to her bed and begins packing.*

JENNY. We are the champions.

AKOUSA. We are champions.

CHARLENE. No time for losers.

ALL. Cos we are the champions.

AKOUSA. Of the worlddddddddddd! Wooo we won.

JENNY. Yes we did.

CHARLENE. Landslide. I can't believe it…

JENNY. Believe it, baby.

AKOUSA. I'm really the Head of the Students' Union.

JENNY. Yes you are.

AKOUSA. I have a job and I'm in control.

CHARLENE. Yep!

AKOUSA. Wow.

She jumps up and down and begins to scream. CHARLENE *joins in with her.*

JENNY. Okay, ladies. Let's get down to business.

AKOUSA *has finished packing. She heads towards the door.*

CHARLENE. Where you going?

AKOUSA. Moving out.

JENNY. Since when?

AKOUSA. Today.

JENNY. We got a few things we need to…

AKOUSA. Thanks for your help but I gonna do this my own way from now on.

JENNY. Pardon me! You need us.

AKOUSA. Not any more. I'm putting together my own team.

CHARLENE. You're firing us!

AKOUSA. The campaign is over.

JENNY. You can't fire us.

AKOUSA. Your services are no longer required.

JENNY. We've worked too hard to be pushed aside now.

AKOUSA. And I am not gonna be pushed about!

JENNY (*to* CHARLENE). Are you hearing what she's saying?

CHARLENE. She's mucking about. (*To* AKOUSA.) How many glasses have you had?

AKOUSA. I'm not drunk.

CHARLENE. Are you being serious?

AKOUSA. You think I didn't know I was being used.

JENNY. Used? What are you on about?

AKOUSA. Joke's on you!

CHARLENE. Stop being silly now!

AKOUSA. It's better to stay quiet and be thought a fool, than to open your mouth and remove all doubt.

JENNY. Meaning…?

AKOUSA. Think about it.

AKOUSA *goes to leave and* JENNY *steps in her way.*

JENNY. You owe me money.

CHARLENE. Yeah.

AKOUSA. You'll get it.

JENNY. I want it now!

AKOUSA. No can do. Have to wait till I get my first pay cheque.

JENNY. You can't leave without giving notice. You won't be getting your deposit back either.

AKOUSA. A loss I can live with.

CHARLENE. Guys!

JENNY. You are not going nowhere until I get my money.

CHARLENE. Let's talk about this reasonably.

JENNY. You know what we can do. I can turn people against you. I built you up and I can tear you down in a heartbeat.

AKOUSA. Go ahead, what you gonna tell 'em. That I didn't pay my rent. I'm a student struggling with my finances, people won't bat an eyelid. Everyone is in the same boat. But I can tell you one thing they don't like, people with hidden agendas. So if I started telling people…

She throws a plastic surgery leaflet at JENNY.

…about you and how you wanted to spend the budget on your boob job, then…

CHARLENE. What, I thought your dad was gonna give you the money…

JENNY. Oh, shut up, Charlene. (*To* AKOUSA.) What exactly were you planning to do with the money, Mrs Goody Two-Shoes. Didn't you have hidden agendas, you just wanted to be popular and you got what you wanted. You don't care about…

AKOUSA. I told you before. I ran because I wanted to make a difference. I am sick and tired of people like you getting away with things because you can. There is gonna be a change around here so you better start getting used to it.

JENNY. Oh, don't make me laugh. Everything is gonna remain the same, you forget we managed your campaign. No way you will ever be able to deliver everything we promised. I'd like to see you try and refurbish the student bar on the budget you have or to make it a four-day week instead of five. So naive, the only power you will ever get is having the title, so if I were you, I would enjoy it while it lasts. Your position is not gonna allow you to start making up rules.

AKOUSA. Shows you don't know much about politics then. Since we started this campaign I've been reading a lot, and you know what I've learnt about the first rule…

CHARLENE. What?

JENNY shoots CHARLENE a look.

AKOUSA. There isn't one.

She leaves the room.

The End.

PINK

Sam Holcroft

Sam Holcroft is currently under commission to the Traverse
Theatre, Clean Break Theatre Company and Paines Plough.
Vanya, Sam's radical adaptation of *Uncle Vanya,* was produced
at the Gate Theatre in 2009. *Cockroach*, co-produced by the
National Theatre of Scotland and the Traverse Theatre, was
nominated for Best New Play by the Critics' Awards 2008 for
Theatre in Scotland, and shortlisted for the John Whiting Award
in 2009. Sam's short play *Vogue* premiered at the Royal Court
Theatre as part of the Angry Now event, and transferred to the
2006 Latitude Festival. In 2009, she was awarded the Tom
Erhardt Award for Up-and-Coming Writers.

Characters

KIM, *thirty-four years, female*
AMY, *twenty-four years, female*
DAN, *thirty-one years, male*
BRIDGET, *fifty-five years, female*

All action takes place in the dressing room of a London television studio.

KIM *finalises her look in one of the mirrors. She is beautifully coiffed and made up.*

There is a knock at the door.

KIM. Come in.

> *The door opens and* AMY *enters carrying cue cards.*

AMY. Hi, sorry to bother you, Ms Keen.

KIM. That's okay. Call me Kim.

AMY. I'm Amy. I've been asked to make sure you have everything you need, Kim?

KIM. I think so.

AMY. Okay, just ask.

> AMY *forces a polite smile.*

> KIM *returns it and then goes back to the mirror.*

Is it alright if we go through some information?

KIM. Sure.

AMY. Tony will introduce you and I just need to check that the details are correct.

KIM. Okay.

AMY. And he's only going to ask you what you're comfortable being asked.

KIM. I know, he said.

AMY. Okay.

> AMY *checks her cue cards.*

So you were born –

> KIM *cuts in.*

KIM. They don't need to know when I was born.

AMY *smiles politely.*

AMY. Sure.

AMY *strikes it from the list.*

And you started in the industry when you were just eighteen?

KIM. Yes. Just.

AMY. And now you're five times Best Picture winner, is that right?

KIM. That is right.

AMY. Congratulations.

KIM. Thank you.

Beat.

AMY. And you now have four production companies.

KIM. That's right, four. It was always my aim to produce and direct and I've been doing that for two years now.

AMY. So you won't ever star in a movie again?

KIM. No, I much prefer my role as producer–director.

AMY *makes a note on the card.*

AMY. He wants to use the word 'entrepreneurial'.

KIM. Sure.

AMY. Because you created your own brand name very early on.

KIM. I did.

AMY. K Play.

KIM. That's right.

AMY. Did you do that on your own?

KIM. Well, who else d'you think did it?

Beat.

AMY. I'm just checking.

KIM. Sure.

Beat.

AMY. Is it true that you have the highest working-women's salary in the industry today?

KIM. I won't comment on that.

AMY. We have it here that you earn an estimated –

KIM. I won't comment on what I earn.

AMY. Can Tony?

KIM. No. We spoke about this previously: he's going to talk about my new product range.

AMY. I have that here.

KIM. That's what we discussed.

AMY. I have it here.

KIM. Good, because that's what I want to talk about, the full range: perfume, clothes, speciality jewellery, sportswear, recipes.

AMY. Recipes?

KIM. Yes.

AMY *nods and makes a note.*

Towels, bed sheets. All with a fifteen per cent discount if you subscribe to the website.

AMY. So you have to be a member?

KIM. Most people are.

AMY. I'm not.

KIM. You're not my demographic.

AMY. No. I'm not.

Beat.

KIM. This is very important, write this down: it launches tomorrow, and our advance orders go out in tomorrow's post. Can you write that down please?

AMY. I don't need to.

KIM. This is very important information, I want you to –

AMY. I have it here already.

    AMY holds up the cue card.

KIM. Okay. Thank you.

    KIM turns back to the mirror.

    AMY continues tentatively.

AMY. As far as Tony's questions about... can you tell us if it's true?

KIM. All our advance orders are confidential so I can't disclose any name or purchase information.

AMY. Can't you even –

KIM. I can't talk about an order specifically, no.

AMY. But would you be happy for us to discuss the possibility of the order?

KIM. Yes, I would.

    AMY smiles politely and makes a note on the cue card.

AMY. And describe the product and what a person would want to do with it if they had ordered it?

KIM. Yes, I have it with me.

AMY. Okay, good, you'll get a close-up and fantastic coverage. Half the nation is going to be watching the programme tonight; we've never had a story this big. This is a lucky break for you.

KIM. I don't consider myself lucky.

    Beat.

AMY. Okay, that's everything, thanks. I'll come back for you in about twenty minutes. Is there anything else you need?

KIM turns to her.

KIM. Yeah, do I look okay?

AMY. Sure. You look the part.

Beat.

AMY turns and exits the room.

KIM stands in silence.

After a moment KIM shrugs off the comment and turns back to the mirror.

There is another knock at the door.

KIM. Just come in, Amy.

The door opens and DAN, a security guard, steps into the room.

Hey –

He looks around the room, checking in the corners and cupboards.

Excuse me? Excuse me? Hello? What are you doing?

Content that the room is safe, he turns to look at KIM, there is a flicker of recognition in his face.

Who are you?

DAN turns and opens the door for BRIDGET to enter. KIM recognises her immediately, and catches her breath.

BRIDGET steps into the room.

BRIDGET. Hello. I'm sorry to arrive unannounced. But this was something of an emergency.

BRIDGET extends her hand.

Bridget Howard. Nice to meet you.

KIM *looks at her, astonished.* BRIDGET *waits with her arm outstretched. Eventually,* KIM *takes her hand.*

KIM. Kim Keen.

They shake hands. They look at one another.

BRIDGET *turns to* DAN.

BRIDGET. Thank you, Dan.

He nods and steps outside, closing the door behind him.

KIM. I –

BRIDGET. When does your interview begin, Kim?

KIM. Twenty minutes.

BRIDGET. Okay.

BRIDGET *checks her watch.*

Have you been interviewed by Tony before?

KIM. No.

BRIDGET. Be careful.

KIM. I'm sorry?

BRIDGET. He interviewed me when I was Foreign Secretary and never again, he had me by the balls inside of five minutes. You must remember it: it was in the papers. Do you read the papers?

KIM. No.

BRIDGET. Well, it was –

KIM. I read *The Economist.*

BRIDGET. Quite right. Then let me tell you, I admitted that my fifteen-year-old daughter was once treated for bulimia. Only a tabloid would fill valuable column inches with a story of a humiliated child and her joyless experience of her young, beautiful body. 'Howard attends Sudanese famine talks while back home daughter binges on Twix bars.' They went through our bins.

Beat.

We all have our moments of weakness, I would only urge you not to have them in front of Tony Edwards.

KIM. I've been through my questions with him.

BRIDGET. So had I.

KIM. I don't have any secrets.

BRIDGET. Everybody has secrets.

KIM. All there is to know about me you can find on the internet.

BRIDGET. Is that right?

KIM. Yes, I've had all the exposure I'm going to get.

Beat.

BRIDGET *unbuttons her coat.*

Excuse me…

BRIDGET. Call me Bridget.

BRIDGET *neatly folds her coat over the back of a chair.*

KIM. I'm afraid I have to finish getting ready.

BRIDGET. Don't let me stop you; we don't have long.

Without missing a beat.

I'm surprised you do your own make-up.

KIM. I always do my own make-up.

BRIDGET. You know best how you need to look.

KIM. I know how I want to look.

BRIDGET. Sure. A lot of time is spent by a lot of people deciding how I should look. A man's wrinkles give him gravitas, but when a woman has a face like crêpe paper she is expected to apologise for herself. People expect her to be ashamed and they enjoy the embarrassment she must feel at no longer being sexually attractive. I still consider myself sexually attractive. Or is it just that I am sexually active?

KIM. Will you not be wanting me to sign a confidentiality agreement?

BRIDGET. No.

KIM. I'm about to go on national television.

BRIDGET. Yes.

KIM. And I could say that I was just in my dressing room with the Prime Minister of Great Britain who told me she was still sexually active.

BRIDGET. Yes. You could.

Beat.

Do you think that would alleviate or aggravate my situation? My not being sexually active would at least provide an acceptable explanation. But for us to be having sex and still he… At least she's good at politics, eh? But what about the tabloids, they'll have a field day: 'While she clearly cannot compensate for her lacking in the Parliamentary Cabinet, he at least can compensate in the bedside cabinet.' You can use that as your own if you like.

KIM *is silent.*

BRIDGET *checks her watch.*

What questions have you agreed to answer?

KIM. We're going to talk about my new product range.

BRIDGET. What questions have you agreed to answer, Kim?

KIM. Where I am not bound by legal confidentiality, I am free to discuss anything I choose.

BRIDGET. Yes, and what will you choose? Legally you cannot name him.

KIM. No.

BRIDGET. And you can't provide proof of purchase.

KIM. I can prove he ordered it.

BRIDGET. Yes, but you cannot show proof of that to the press.

KIM. No.

BRIDGET. But you could confirm the authenticity of the leaked purchase order if it was shown to you?

KIM. Yes.

BRIDGET *pulls a folded photocopy out of her coat pocket and passes it to* KIM.

BRIDGET. Is this a true copy of the original?

KIM *takes the photocopy.*

Did your company, K Play, issue this receipt?

KIM. Yes.

BRIDGET. It is not a fake?

KIM. No.

BRIDGET. Are you sure?

KIM. Yes.

Beat.

BRIDGET *takes the receipt back, folding it and placing it back in her coat pocket.*

KIM *watches her, on edge.*

BRIDGET. This is a good opportunity for you.

KIM. I wouldn't call it that.

BRIDGET. What would you call it?

KIM. I work hard; I'm a businesswoman.

BRIDGET. Exactly: an opportunist.

KIM. If that's what you think.

BRIDGET. This is a superb piece of free marketing for you and I also expect they are paying you handsomely for your time this evening. And that's fine; I admire that. I am pro-business, pro-enterprise. We have an economy to rebuild and I have pledged to support hard-working industrialists. So long as they pay their taxes.

Beat.

KIM. You can't stop me from promoting my product.

BRIDGET. That's true. Legally I can't.

KIM. It's not my fault that your husband –

BRIDGET. How long has he been a member?

KIM. I don't know.

BRIDGET. Don't tell me you don't know.

KIM. I don't.

BRIDGET. You can't build an empire on an empty brain. The first thing you would have done when this hit the headlines was to discover the legitimacy of the claim.

KIM. I can't disclose that information.

BRIDGET. I'm the Prime Minister, you tell me for how long my husband has subscribed to your pornography cartel.

Beat.

KIM. Three years ago in January.

BRIDGET. January?

KIM. Yes.

BRIDGET. After Christmas.

Pause.

What else has he purchased from you?

KIM. The product range was only available for advance sales two months ago.

BRIDGET. And so what else has he purchased from you?

KIM. Up until now he has only ever bought films.

BRIDGET. Just films?

KIM. He exclusively watches the movies and that's all.

BRIDGET. Movies of you?

KIM. Yes.

BRIDGET. How many?

KIM. Every one.

Beat.

BRIDGET. Will you pass me that newspaper, please?

KIM *passes her the newspaper.* BRIDGET *looks at the picture on the front page.*

I told him not to cover his face with his hands – he's not a criminal.

She turns the pages to find a particular opinion piece.

Here. Did you read this one yet? Of course, you don't read the papers.

BRIDGET *reads –*

'While I find myself simultaneously recoiling in disgust and sniggering behind my fingers, I also can't help feeling a little sympathy: would my husband not do the same if I forced him to share our bed with my lizard-skin handbag…'

BRIDGET *half smiles. She folds the newspaper shut.*

I have to be just as secure in my policies as I am in my physical appearance to weather the criticism. But I will admit it never ceases to surprise me that the critics are so often women.

KIM *shifts uneasily.*

We have a lot to learn from men. They have always been better at supporting one another than we women have.

KIM. I've made my way without –

BRIDGET *cuts across her.*

BRIDGET. There are three types of women in politics. I'd be interested to see if it's the same for pornography. You can tell me. Three types. One: the sexually alluring schemer, I'd say that's true for both, wouldn't you?

KIM *is silent.*

Two: the patriarch in a dress. Same again? Different dress. And three… well, you tell me, because we haven't made our mind up on that one yet. Everybody's after lucky number three, aren't they? And we can't tell you exactly what she'll be like, but we can certainly tell you what she won't be like… she certainly won't be too ugly, God no, but then she can't be too pretty either. And she won't be simple-minded, but then she can't be too high-achieving because that casts our own achievements in a dull light. So just so long as she's modest, but we don't want to be embarrassed by her so… but then, hang on, no, I tell you what, we'll know it when we see it.

BRIDGET *smiles again.*

We don't have a third type in politics. But if there were a third type in your industry, I'd put my money on it being you.

KIM *is silent.*

It must take courage to enter your profession.

KIM. Not really.

BRIDGET. No?

KIM. I was dancing in clubs, moving into films was almost natural.

BRIDGET. The move from dancing to…

KIM. Sex, yes. Especially when you were having sex for cash in the clubs.

Beat.

BRIDGET *checks her watch, she ploughs on.*

BRIDGET. How many films do you appear in a year?

KIM. I'm retired; I don't act any more.

BRIDGET. When you were acting, how many?

KIM. Four.

> BRIDGET *is concerned by this*.

BRIDGET. Only four?

KIM. Never more than that, no.

BRIDGET. Why?

KIM. Because.

BRIDGET. Why?

KIM. Because I…

BRIDGET. Tell me.

KIM. I get sore.

> *Beat*.

BRIDGET. Do your customers know that?

KIM. I'm sorry?

BRIDGET. Do your customers know that you only made four films a year because to do more would damage your vagina? Do they know that?

KIM. Of course they don't.

BRIDGET. Of course. Because you create an alternate world for them, don't you? A world where you cannot rub a woman raw.

KIM. That's not what I said.

BRIDGET. A world where beautiful, gentle women are willing and able to enjoy their subservience.

KIM. That's not how it is.

BRIDGET. You don't see it that way?

KIM. No.

BRIDGET. I haven't seen your movies so you'll have to tell me
– do you ever turn around and say, 'No, stop doing that, it's
not working for me'? Do you? Do you ever say, 'Actually, I
don't think I can orgasm in this position, sorry'?

The two women meet eyes.

You tell me how it works. Are you not willing and able to
express pleasure when they stretch you wide open? When
they scratch at you? When they pull on your hair? Yes or no?

KIM *doesn't respond.*

Simple question, even when they urinate on you and
sodomise you –

KIM. I haven't done that in a long time.

BRIDGET. – do you or do you not still look up at them with
semen all over your face and gaze in deference. To The Man?

Beat.

KIM. I don't have to listen to this.

BRIDGET. Then let's have a conversation.

KIM. They come to me in their millions.

BRIDGET. Yes, if I had a penis and a sense of powerlessness, I
too would come to you.

KIM. For intimacy, that's what they come looking for.

BRIDGET. They come because it's easy.

KIM. They come to me for the intimacy they are missing at
home. And sometimes they are so deprived of it that they go
out of their way to get caught.

BRIDGET. You'd be wise to remember who you're talking to.

KIM. Sometimes an 'accident' is actually a cry for attention.

BRIDGET. My relationship with my –

KIM *half laughs.*

KIM. Claiming for a sex toy on expenses is quite an accident! You don't think that maybe –

BRIDGET. No.

KIM. – just maybe he wanted to be found out?

BRIDGET. Don't presume to know a thing about my husband.

KIM. I know he owns my entire collection.

BRIDGET. That doesn't mean –

KIM. And a man who watches more than one hundred movies of the same woman must be a man searching for connection.

BRIDGET. Please, don't flatter yourself, you are less than a whore to him, you are a fucking cartoon character!

Pause.

You broke confidentiality, Kim. Just now. You understand that? By telling me the details of my husband's membership.

KIM. But I... You're the Prime Minister.

BRIDGET. It makes no difference. You still breached the contract you have with your customer. It's alright, you didn't break the law, you can't be prosecuted for it but my husband could sue you. To be prosecuted you'd have to have done something illegal. Have you ever done anything illegal?

KIM. What?

BRIDGET. Say, having sex for cash in the clubs?

Beat.

KIM. That was the club's liability, not mine. You're trying to find a way to blackmail me so I won't do the show. I don't care about your husband, alright, I've got a product range to launch, that's why I'm here. I've been campaigning for a year now about the state of my industry.

BRIDGET. I've noticed.

KIM. And you did nothing. Illegal downloads are killing my sales. I can't compete with user-generated free porn coming out of people's bedrooms. The entire industry is being crushed, but you do nothing because you don't want to get your hands dirty. And so what do I have to do to stop my business sinking like a lead shit? I have to diversify. I have to create a whole new range of products and this is my opportunity, my big opportunity to advertise and you want to take that away from me. You have some nerve coming in here and calling yourself pro-enterprise.

BRIDGET. Do you have it?

KIM. There's a word for that kind of behaviour.

BRIDGET. Relax, Kim. Can I see it? I assume you have it here?

Beat.

Please?

BRIDGET *checks her watch while* KIM *reaches for a box tied with ribbon. She passes it to* BRIDGET. BRIDGET *takes the box, places it on the side and undoes the ribbon. She lifts the lid off the box and takes out a black-velvet pouch.*

A lot goes into the packaging.

KIM. We tend to use black for men.

BRIDGET. And for women?

KIM. Pink.

BRIDGET. Of course.

BRIDGET *puts her hand inside the velvet pouch and stiffens slightly. She withdraws her hand, pulling out a pink silicone vagina with pubic hair. She looks at it for a long time.*

So this is yours?

KIM. Yes.

BRIDGET. Modelled on yours?

KIM. Moulded to mine and recreated in silicone.

BRIDGET. Is this your pubic hair?

KIM. No.

BRIDGET. Whose pubic hair is this?

KIM. It's synthetic hair.

BRIDGET. It's not real?

KIM. No, but it's designed to look as real as possible.

BRIDGET. It's effective.

KIM. Thank you.

> *Beat.*

> BRIDGET *examines it closely.*

> Try it.

BRIDGET. Excuse me?

KIM. Why don't you try it? Feel inside it.

> BRIDGET *looks at it. She is about to stick her fingers inside when* KIM *offers her some lubricant.*

> You should lubricate your fingers.

> *Instead of taking the tube,* BRIDGET *offers* KIM *her fingers.* KIM *squeezes lubricant onto* BRIDGET'S *fingers and liberally covers them.*

> BRIDGET *inserts her fingers into the silicone vagina, businesslike at first then softening with curiosity.* BRIDGET *looks at* KIM *searching for answers.*

> KIM *shrugs in a moment of conciliation.*

> They watch my movie, fuck my pussy.

> BRIDGET *looks back at the vagina. She withdraws her fingers and places it back in the box.* KIM *hands her a tissue;* BRIDGET *wipes her fingers.*

BRIDGET. It is demeaning to my husband for him to have to come up onstage and kiss me after a big speech. So we just take each other's hands and raise them high instead.

BRIDGET *discards the tissue.*

You know my husband has watched pornography all his life. Despite what everybody might think, this isn't news to me.

BRIDGET *smiles, ruefully.*

Even before his first sexual relationship – way before – he was reading pornographic magazines in the toilets at boarding school. Now of course it's not magazines, it's movies – your movies – in schools.

KIM. You have to be over eighteen to subscribe.

BRIDGET. It's been my experience that age restrictions on luxury items are hard to enforce.

KIM *doesn't retaliate.*

You understand that pornography – your pornography – is now the Great British sex education? Hoards of young, lonely, insecure schoolboys looking for unconditionally accepting women to act as surrogate mothers. And what does it teach them? It teaches them that sex is for the purpose of what a man can do to a woman. And isn't that so very reassuring? There's no criticism, there's no being laughed at, or talked about behind your back, there's no embarrassment, just eager, eager women who are bending over themselves to please.

KIM. They are curious.

BRIDGET *cuts across her.*

BRIDGET. But then they graduate, they go out into the world with the illusion that this is a woman's rightful place and that she is no challenge to male authority. And when they realise in their daily life that this is not in fact the case, it's devastating for them, do you understand that? Devastating. And what do they do with that confusion and that anger? They beat their wives and mistrust their mothers and find it almost impossible to relate to real women of flesh and blood. It is not just your vagina, Kim, but society that is damaged by what you do.

KIM *smiles.*

KIM. Did you really come here to lecture me? Did you think one conversation with the Great British Prime Minister would move me to rethink everything that I have come to believe about what I do? What, in the hopes that I won't put this – (*She motions to the silicone vagina.*) before your Great British public? Unless you are willing to talk about drawing up a legitimate stimulus plan for my industry then I see no reason why I should have to miss out on this marketing opportunity. I'm sorry, but I only have ten minutes before I have to appear on a television show –

BRIDGET. I only have ten minutes before I have to appear before the Iranian Ambassador to discuss anti-terror legislation so don't think I am not aware of the time pressure here.

Beat.

For someone who so readily complains about the state of her industry, I am surprised you have managed to stay afloat so long. I commend you.

KIM. I have diversified.

BRIDGET. Only recently.

KIM. It's a robust business.

BRIDGET. Your investors are loyal to you.

KIM. Yes.

BRIDGET. I met Sacha Ignatova; I wasn't aware that he had moved to London.

KIM. Yes.

BRIDGET. He is your main investor?

KIM. No.

BRIDGET. He has only a forty-nine per cent stake. He mentioned.

KIM doesn't respond.

The British Ambassador to the Ukraine has been on the
phone with me this morning; he is a close friend of Choma
Markowski. He is your main investor?

KIM *smiles*.

KIM. They are aware of the situation.

BRIDGET. So I hear.

KIM. Choma was my first phone call. And we laughed about it.
In fact he suggested it would be a good story for a film. He
makes a fortune from my sales, there's no chance he would
feel pressurised by the Prime Minister of a country that
means nothing to him.

BRIDGET. He is a forty-nine per cent stakeholder also, no?
Leaving you only two per cent in your own company.

KIM. My investors would never abandon me; I have no reason
to feel threatened by you.

BRIDGET. But for years I thought that the pride of our British
pornography would not have in fact made it without the
championship of American money. I was certain that Brent
Matthison had part ownership of your company.

KIM. You don't want me on that TV show, then make me an
offer. If you want to talk about a stimulus package for my
industry then I'd be happy to meet you with my financial
director.

BRIDGET. I know Brent well, Kim. He will answer his phone
to me in a heartbeat and I am pretty sure that he has more
than a two per cent share in a business that he helped build
from nothing.

KIM *bristles and picks up her handbag*.

KIM. You think I haven't had people treat me like this my
whole life: suspicious, patronising, avoiding me in the street,
being embarrassed to have me as a friend. I've worked
harder than anyone I know to be in a position not to have to
be treated like a criminal.

BRIDGET. You have worked hard.

KIM. Harder than anyone I know.

BRIDGET. And all you worked to build was beginning to crumble around you.

KIM. I diversified.

BRIDGET. Your investors were losing their money, your savings were disappearing; you were on the brink of collapse.

KIM. I diversified!

BRIDGET. Yes, and how did you raise the capital for diversification, Kim?

Beat.

KIM. How dare you accuse me of –

BRIDGET. You had no capital, Kim.

KIM. I don't have to listen to this.

KIM *is about to brush past* BRIDGET.

BRIDGET. Investment fraud is a crime.

KIM *stops.*

Five years minimum. Twenty-five maximum.

KIM *and* BRIDGET *look at one another.*

KIM. You have no proof.

BRIDGET. If I call Brent Matthison right now on this phone – (*She motions to the green-room telephone.*) he won't confirm for me that you also sold him forty-nine per cent of your company in early 2000? Now, I'm no mathematician, Kimberly, but I even I know that three forty-nines do not add up to one hundred.

Beat.

And I'm willing to bet that not far under the surface of your financial reporting, I'll find more than three.

KIM. Think seriously about what you're suggesting.

BRIDGET. I have.

KIM. You've thought about the effect it will have on the industry?

BRIDGET. Your contemporaries will endeavor to keep their finances above-board, I'm sure.

KIM. I've worked twice as hard as any man in my industry to get to where I am. I fired my management, I ran my own affairs, I acted on my own ideas and I make my own decisions. Do you know how rare that is?

BRIDGET. I do.

KIM. I am completely in control of every endorsement, of every brand that carries my name. When I sit down for a business meeting I never leave the room.

BRIDGET *nods*.

A decision doesn't get made unless I'm there.

BRIDGET. It's the only way.

KIM. In my last three movies I did no anal. Okay? No anal.

BRIDGET. Okay.

KIM. That's unheard of. And they were still the highest-grossing films of the year. I have paved the way for women coming behind me, I have made it okay for them to choose what they do and don't want to do. I have empowered them.

BRIDGET *nods again*.

They are calling the shots because of me and you want to remove my influence? You want to take really the only powerful woman that works in that dog kennel of an industry and lock her up? So, what, schoolboys won't buy my movies any more? They're just going to go and buy somebody else's and the women in those films will be made to do a lot worse than in mine. Have you seen any of the user-generated content coming out of Eastern Europe? It's not pretty. I think some of the girls might not be there out of choice, know what I'm saying? And you want to erase my presence in the Ukraine? You take me out the picture and you open the canopy for low-cost, unregulated, dirty – I mean, under-the-fingernails dirty – porn to rise up and take my place. And they'll swarm to it like bees to honey, cos it comes free. You want to lose that revenue? Big money we make, more money than Hollywood: jobs, manufacturing, hard-working, productive people all feeding your economy.

BRIDGET. I understand that.

KIM. You don't understand that, you want to return my industry to the Dark Ages. We practise clean, safe sex; our girls are routinely tested, supported emotionally and financially to the tune of the hundreds of thousands. And you question why I had to save my business.

BRIDGET. I understand that you were under pressure.

KIM. You have no idea.

BRIDGET. I don't understand pressure?

KIM. You don't know the meaning of hard work until you've had to fuck for your living.

BRIDGET. You built a truly remarkable business.

KIM. And now you want me to rot in jail.

BRIDGET. When it collapsed, you panicked.

KIM. So I can be photographed with a face like crêpe paper and your husband won't want to fuck me any more. He's just going to want to fuck some sixteen-year-old Slovakian pussy instead.

BRIDGET. You were trying to save your business, I know.

KIM. And you can find her and bang her up too.

BRIDGET. I know you were only trying to be clever, Kim.

KIM (*spitting the words*). Fuck you!

Pause.

KIM *breathes deeply.*

BRIDGET *checks her watch, she wrings her hands.*

BRIDGET. Let me explain something to you, can I?

KIM *paces.*

Kim? When I needed to change legislation on sex crime I put the issue in the mouth of Alan Hedger, Secretary of Education. Because people don't need to hear it from me, a woman, they need to hear it from a man. Are you listening to me? While I am talking about the armed forces and the NHS, a fifteen-stone man of six foot three inches in height is visiting secondary schools and talking to children about sexual violence. So that boys will learn that not all girls are willing to be handled aggressively.

Beat.

I delegate. I delegate to people whom the public will better accept. It makes me a lot more effective. Kim, I don't want to take away your business.

KIM *looks at her, confused.*

And I would rather not see you in jail for the rest of your working life. It would be a criminal waste of resources.

KIM. I don't...

BRIDGET. Rather than see the collapse of the empire you worked so hard to build I would like to draw on those resources, Kim, I would like to delegate to you.

KIM. What do you mean?

BRIDGET. You are one of the most powerful porn stars in the world. You have the global sex industry in your hands and this...

BRIDGET *picks up the silicone vagina and holds it up for her.*

...this is what you do with it.

Beat.

Help me.

KIM. Help you?

BRIDGET *returns the silicone vagina to its box.*

BRIDGET. There are very few women in this country who are as powerful as I am. Yes, I want you to help me.

KIM. I… I don't… What do you want?

BRIDGET. I want you to come out of retirement.

KIM. What?

BRIDGET. That's what I want.

KIM. You want me to make more movies?

BRIDGET. Yes.

KIM. I'm thirty-three.

BRIDGET. It doesn't matter.

KIM. Nobody wants to see a thirty-three-year-old fucking any more.

BRIDGET. You still look the part, Kim.

KIM. I've had a child.

She points at the silicone vagina.

My vagina doesn't look like that these days.

BRIDGET. There are surgeries.

KIM. I don't want to make movies any more.

BRIDGET. I need you to make movies, Kim.

KIM. I built my business so that I wouldn't have to always make movies.

BRIDGET. I need you to influence the way movies will be made. You're in charge, Kim, you are in a position to make change.

KIM. Change?

BRIDGET. Subtle, subtle change. Things must be done gently, ever so gently. We must be gently led, and subtly educated in the art of equality. How? You are going to make equality sexy.

KIM. What?

BRIDGET. Listen to me, you are going to gradually pull the focus away from male pleasure towards mutual pleasure. You are going to slowly tailor your films, for both men *and* women. You need to balance the power play.

KIM. Do you mean S&M?

BRIDGET. No, no, because even with S&M the woman ends up trussed in latex with multiple partners.

KIM. I thought you said you never saw my movies.

BRIDGET. We're talking about fucking them in the arse.

KIM. You want me to fuck them in the arse?

BRIDGET. Subtly. Very subtly, so they don't even know how it got there. And the situations, little by little the situations must change.

KIM. What do you mean?

BRIDGET. Usually it's a woman whose car has broken down, right? A woman who's hitchhiking or she is the stranger at a party – any number of situations where the woman is vulnerable and so grateful of rescue that she is willing to be gangbanged by five overweight balding men. No, I'm talking different scenarios.

BRIDGET *checks her watch*.

The *man's* car has broken down. The *man* can't fix his computer. The *man* is making coffee for his boss, his bigbreasted boss. Women like to watch movies with storylines, they want their movies to be artistic, passionate, emotionally engaging. Less porn; more erotica.

KIM. Men will never buy it.

BRIDGET. Yes they will, if the change is so subtle as to be almost imperceptible. We'll have them thinking it was their idea. And think of the next generation: if you eat vegetables when you are young, Kim, you will always like vegetables and you will always be healthier. And what's more, women will begin to like you. You will release a book: a girl's guide to sex.

KIM. A what…?

BRIDGET. That's it, get women to like you, and women will welcome your pornography into their homes and relationships.

KIM. You want women to watch my porn?

BRIDGET. Yes, I want women to watch lots and lots of porn! I want women to bring your porn into their bedrooms and watch it with their boyfriends, their husbands. I want men to begin associating this kind of porn with fulfilling, successful sex. I want them to see their women aroused and empowered and find it exciting. I want them to leave the bedroom and look for it in the boardroom.

KIM. Sex?

BRIDGET. No, equality. You're not listening to me, it is not about getting the upper hand, it's about being even-handed. Do you understand what I am asking you to do? Kim?

KIM. I don't… I don't think…

BRIDGET. I need you to make lots more movies.

KIM. I never do more than four movies a year.

BRIDGET. I need you to make more movies than that.

KIM. I can't.

BRIDGET. Yes you can.

KIM. I get sore; I can't have sex with my husband.

BRIDGET. I will see to it that you have the best gynaecologist.

KIM. I don't need –

BRIDGET. It's not for long.

KIM. How long?

BRIDGET. Six years, maybe seven.

KIM. Seven years!

BRIDGET. Compared with twenty-five in prison it's a mild sentence.

Beat.

BRIDGET *checks her watch and reaches for her coat.*

KIM. No.

BRIDGET *stops.*

No.

BRIDGET. Think seriously, Kim.

KIM. This is… this is bullshit.

BRIDGET *lays her coat back down, wipes her mouth.*

Put your coat on, no way I'm doing this. I'm not making this crap, nobody will buy this crap, are you serious? I make good porn, great porn; I am an *expert*! My porn is fantastic – cathartic, exciting; it lowers the inhibitions and tensions of millions and millions of –

BRIDGET. Men.

KIM. I don't have to sell it to you; I don't have to prove its benefits for its right to exist. You say I damage society, but what about smoking, what about smoking and drinking? Or are you blackmailing the makers of cigarettes as well? If people, free from coercion, want to film themselves fucking each other, and other people, also free from coercion, want to pay to see it, well, I was led to believe that in a free society no one could stand in their way. It's the freedom that's important, not what people do with it. How can you call yourself a leader of a democracy and censor my right to create?

BRIDGET. We don't have time to argue this, Kim.

KIM. Then leave me alone.

KIM *picks up the silicone vagina and puts it back in the packaging.*

BRIDGET. I'm not bluffing, Kim.

KIM. Neither am I.

BRIDGET. I will call the Serious Fraud Office the moment I leave this room.

KIM *turns on her.*

KIM. You'll be tied up in investigations for years and even then we'll settle!

BRIDGET *nods.*

BRIDGET. Yes, it will be costly and time-consuming.

KIM. And by then this business with your husband will be over and done.

BRIDGET. But knowing his reputation, I could not guarantee that Choma Markowski would leave your punishment in the hands of the British Criminal Justice System.

Beat.

KIM *turns to her, real fear in her eyes.*

Believe I have no qualms in doing it, Kim. I would not be the leader of a democracy without having done worse many times before.

KIM. I have a daughter.

BRIDGET. So do I.

There is a knock at the door.

AMY. Ms Keen?

BRIDGET *and* KIM *look at one another in alarm.*

KIM. Just a second, Amy.

AMY. We're ready for you, Ms Keen.

KIM. I'll be out in a minute.

AMY. Alright, but we don't have long.

BRIDGET *stares at* KIM.

KIM *racks her brain for a solution.*

BRIDGET (*urgently*). All I am asking is that you go on this television show and announce that you will be coming out of retirement because you miss it and you know that you have so much more to give.

KIM. I have to go.

KIM *makes to move towards the door.*

BRIDGET. Kim, Kim, listen to me, I am asking you to use your power. (*With great urgency.*) I will never overcome this incident. It will dog me the rest of my political life.

KIM *stops at the door.*

It will be in every newspaper headline, every time I try to implement some change, however small, they will drag it up again and use it against me. I won't be remembered for what I have tried to do for my country, I'll be remembered for the fact that my husband needs a plastic vagina because I have a dick in these trousers. For them to be ready and willing to accept this third kind of woman we must make change. We must create an alternate world, one in which you and I are not out of the ordinary.

BRIDGET *stands, slightly breathless.*

Kim?

KIM *turns to her, they look at one another.*

KIM *looks down at the box containing the silicone vagina.*

KIM. Our advance orders go out in tomorrow's post. This one belongs to your husband. Perhaps you could deliver it yourself.

KIM *offers the box to* BRIDGET. BRIDGET *takes the box. They look at one another a final time before* KIM *turns and exits the room.*

BRIDGET *stands with the box. The lights fade.*

The End.

YOU, ME AND Wii

Sue Townsend

Sue Townsend won the Thames Television Playwright Award for her debut play *Womberang*. Her subsequent writing for the stage includes *The Great Celestial Cow*, *Ten Tiny Fingers, Nine Tiny Toes* and most recently *Are You Sitting Comfortably*? She is best known for her series of books about Adrian Mole. *The Secret Diary of Adrian Mole Aged 13 ¾*, *Adrian Mole: The Wilderness Years* and *Adrian Mole*: *The Cappuccino Years* have all been serialised for radio. Townsend adapted *The Cappucino Years* for television as well as adapting several of her books for the stage, including *The Queen and I*.

Characters

VINCENT, *early twenties*
SHEILA, *mid-sixties*
KERRY, *thirty-five*
COURTNEY, *fourteen*
SELINA, *forties*
MARK

*A living room on a local-authority sink estate. An old 'modern'
sofa and matching armchair. A large flat-screen television on
the wall. A man in his early twenties, VINCENT, skiing on a
Wii. A woman in her mid-sixties, SHEILA, is in an armchair
feeding McKenzie, a baby girl. KERRY, thirty-five, is kneeling
on the carpet ironing baby clothes. COURTNEY, fourteen, the
baby's mother, is on MSN Messenger on the computer. They are
all wearing dressing gowns and slippers. It is three o'clock in
the afternoon.*

COURTNEY. Mam, Lisa Lovett has just called me a slapper.

KERRY. Tell her you can't be a slapper at fourteen; you have to
be in your forties before somebody can call you a slapper.

COURTNEY. She says I'm too young to be a proper mother.

SHEILA. She's right. Why is *your* mam on *her* hands and knees
ironing *your* baby's clothes?

COURTNEY. Because the ironing board's broke.

VINCENT. You're an idle cow, Courtney.

COURTNEY. No! I were helping Mam bath her this morning!
She gave us this big smile, didn't she, Mam? And she looked
like a proper person, she did, didn't she, Mam?

KERRY. Well…

COURTNEY. Since she's been here, everything has changed.
She's made everything better since she was put on the earth.

KERRY. Alright, Courtney, McKenzie is lovely an' that but she
ain't the New Messiah. She ain't even a person.

COURTNEY. Do you know why we're here, Nan?

SHEILA. No I don't, Courtney, Google it.

KERRY. People are born, people die, and there's this bit inbetween.

VINCENT (*to everybody*). I've just done a run in twenty point five!

SHEILA (*disinterested*). Right.

She puts McKenzie on her shoulder to wind her. She croons and rocks with the baby.

Come on, my little one. Bring your wind up for your nana.

The doorbell rings. Everybody tenses – visitors are not welcome. Doorbell rings again. They all look towards the front door.

(*To* KERRY.) It's the loan bloke. We should never have took out that loan. He's the only one what goes on that bloody Wii.

The letter box is rattled.

Go and look out the window, Courtney.

COURTNEY *goes out to look. Everybody waits tensely for* COURTNEY.

COURTNEY. There's a woman and man at the doorstep. The woman's covered in blood.

SHEILA *holds the baby protectively and goes to the corner of the room.*

SHEILA. Where there's blood there's trouble.

KERRY. Tell 'em to fuck off!

SELINA (*off*). Mrs Lamb, Selina Snow, your Member of Parliament. Can I come in?

The family don't move or speak.

SHEILA. Let her in, Courtney.

Everybody does a quick tidy-up.

COURTNEY (*off*). Nana says to go in. She's in the front room.

SELINA, *in her forties, attractive, dressed in a cream suit which is spattered with blood. She is holding a bloodied tissue to her forehead. A young man from Millbank,* MARK, *has an arm around* SELINA. *He is speaking into his mobile.* SELINA *and* MARK *are wearing Labour Party rosettes.*

SHEILA *hands the baby to* COURTNEY *and takes the shocked* SELINA *to the armchair and gently forces her to sit down.*

SHEILA. What the bloody hell happened to you?

SELINA. They hate me out there! They're tearing my leaflets up in front of me!

MARK (*into phone*). Toby. We've got a Jackie O situation here. A troglodyte in a skiing hat has just lobbed a can of White Lightning at Selina's head.

Pause.

Do we want photographs of Selina Snow with her nice Jaeger suit covered in blood on the six o'clock?

Pause.

He disconnects the phone.

(*To* SELINA.) They're ringing back.

SELINA. It's so unfair! I've done so much work on the Youth and Justice Bill!

SHEILA. I'll fetch a bowl of water and a flannel.

MARK *raises his hand to stop* SHEILA *from leaving the room and shouts.*

MARK. Wait!

SHEILA. Mr Manners forgot to call on you today, didn't he? (*To* SELINA.) Do you want a cup of tea, duck?

SELINA. No. I have some water in my bag.

She takes out a bottle of Evian water.

Do you have a clean glass?

KERRY. I'll clear the ferrets out of the glass cupboard and see, shall I?

KERRY *goes out.*

SHEILA. Who chucked the can at you?

COURTNEY. Lee Adkins drinks White Lightning.

VINCENT. Lee Adkins wunt chuck a full can. He's an alky.

SELINA. The can was full of small stones. It was obviously premeditated.

MARK (*to* SELINA). Stand up, Selina. I need to get a good shot of the blood.

SHEILA *helps* SELINA *to stand.* MARK *holds his Black-Berry up and takes a picture.*

(*To* SHEILA.) You can clean her up now.

SHEILA (*shouting*). Kerry, bowl and flannel, while you're in there.

SELINA *starts to cry.*

Don't cry, duck.

SELINA. I never cry. Never. Can't remember the last time. My sister sent me a text halfway through Prime Minister's Questions to tell me my mother had died, I didn't cry then. I was sitting behind Gordon in full shot of the cameras but I kept my composure. Perhaps I should have gone to view the body but I was chairing a committee on Families and Health. It's alright for my sister. All she does is sit on her fat arse all day eating After Eights, and watching that dreadful Jeremy Kyle.

SHEILA. What did ya mam die of?

SELINA. I've forgotten. Obviously something fatal.

SHEILA. You cried when you won your seat for the first time, I were there at the count. I 'ad such hopes.

SELINA. When I left the community centre the air was full of May blossom.

A cock crows. It is MARK*'s ringtone.*

The family laugh.

MARK (*on the phone*). So how do we play it?

Pause.

Selina Snow, Junior Minister for blah blah-dy blah attack by yob or mob?

KERRY *comes in with a glass, a bowl and a flannel.*

MARK *carries on nodding and saying –*

Yeah… right…

KERRY. Lee Adkins is fat but even he ain't a mob.

SHEILA. He wunt have been with any kind of mob. He hasn't got any friends.

COURTNEY. He still shits himself.

SHEILA *passes McKenzie to* COURTNEY.

SHEILA. Don't go chucking her up and down. She's just had her bottle.

She dips the flannel in the bowl and starts to wipe the blood from SELINA*'s head.*

SELINA. Is it bad? Will I need stitches? Will it leave a scar?

SHEILA. No. It just needs one of them butterfly clips. We've got loads of them.

KERRY. I used to clean at the hospital.

SHEILA. She used to come home with her pockets full of bandages and stuff.

KERRY. The doctors and nurses used to nick owt, so why wouldn't I?

SELINA. No wonder the NHS is on its knees.

MARK. Where the fuck are the police?

Everyone in the room laughs loudly apart from MARK *and* SELINA, *who look baffled.*

SHEILA. You're living in the past, duck.

KERRY. You should have said it were a gang of Somalians. That brings the coppers out of their hidey-holes.

MARK *goes over to* VINCENT, *who is skiing again.*

MARK. What's your best time?

VINCENT. I've just done forty-seven on the downhill.

MARK. Not bad.

VINCENT *passes* MARK *a controller and they begin to ski together.*

SHEILA. I'd love to send Vincent real skiing. Somewhere proper, like Dubai.

SELINA. May I ask you why you're still in your dressing gowns at three o'clock in the afternoon? Have you just woken up or are you about to go to bed?

SHEILA. There's no point in getting dressed. We don't go out.

SELINA. What, none of you? What about food?

KERRY. Iceland deliver it.

SELINA (*to* COURTNEY). But you must go to school?

COURTNEY (*proudly*). No, I'm a full-time homemaker.

KERRY (*sarcastically*). Yeah, I wish.

SELINA. How old are you?

COURTNEY. I'm fourteen and a half.

SELINA. But you could still go to school.

COURTNEY. I didn't like it. The lads wouldn't let you do your work, right? The teachers were always away with stress and nervous breakdowns, right?

SHEILA (*scornfully*). Stress! They don't know what stress is. It were a lovely school when I were there. There were flower beds and cloths on the tables at dinner time. I never had a day off. I went with pneumonia once. I passed my 11 Plus, I were the only one in our street. The bloke in the newsagents gave me a double box of Black Magic. Oh, I did feel special! Me dad took the letter to work to show his mates.

KERRY (*to* SELINA). She could have gone to the grammar but there were no money for the uniform.

SHEILA. It were the extras: leather satchel…

The family join in. This is a familiar story.

Hockey boots, hockey skirt, hockey stick, netball skirt, Aertex tops. Tennis skirt, tennis shoes, tennis racket, straw hat for summer, black beret for winter, fountain pen, ruler, set square, compasses…

The family shout.

Gym knickers!

The family laugh.

It were one way of keeping the clever riff-raff out.

SELINA. But you must go to school, Courtney.

COURTNEY. I can't. I don't like it out there.

KERRY. There's nothing to go out for.

VINCENT (*still skiing*). It's better in home.

SELINA. But there are CCTV cameras everywhere on the estate. I was instrumental in finding the money.

SHEILA. They're as useful as a condom on a limp dick! There's no film in the cameras! You're on your own out there.

SELINA (*to* COURTNEY). Do you read?

COURTNEY. I could read when I were six.

SELINA. But do you read now?

COURTNEY. Course I can. You don't forget how to read.

SHEILA. We used to have a neighbour that brought us books.

KERRY. Till the library closed.

SELINA. Are you still a Party member, Sheila?

SHEILA. Oh no. Not since Wayne next door had two legs and an arm blown off. Have you seen him lately?

SELINA. No, not since the hospital.

KERRY. Yeah, we heard about that. His mam chucked you out, didn't she? Cos you voted for the war.

SELINA. She was distraught… I can understand that. I have children myself.

COURTNEY. His mam brings him round 'ere in his wheelchair sometimes. He's always asking if he can hold the baby, but I won't let him.

Slight pause.

Not with the one arm.

MARK. No, you couldn't trust a triple amputee.

SHEILA. That suit's ruined. Take it off and give it to Kerry. She's good with bloodstains.

KERRY. I were married to a maniac.

SELINA *takes her skirt and jacket off. She is wearing a very beautiful underslip.* KERRY *takes her dressing gown off and gives it to* SELINA *to wear.* KERRY *is wearing a long T-shirt that she slept in. She goes off with the suit.* SELINA *sits down tucking her legs beneath her.*

SELINA. God, this feels so nice! I hate canvassing. Can I rely on your vote, Sheila?

SHEILA. I'm not being funny, Mrs Snow, but I think I'm going to wait until Old Labour come back. I can't get on with New.

SELINA's phone rings. She answers it.

SELINA. Tess! Did you have a lovely day darling…? Why, what happened?

As SELINA *listens she becomes more upset.*

But Daddy was meant to pick you up. I can't, I'm in Leicester, canvassing.

Raising voice.

I'm two and a half hours away, darling. Let me speak to Miss Bell…

Pause.

Miss Bell, I'm terribly sorry about… My husband was meant to… Yes, I'll ring him now.

She speed dials.

Where the fuck are you? You're meant to be picking Tess up… You are… I'm in Leicester! You'll have to leave the meeting. Tess is in bits! No, the school won't 'put her in a car' –

Pause.

Because the school's not insured should Tess be murdered and we sue… Howard, *please* pick her up… For Christ's sake, it's not as though your meeting's important! You import teddy bears from China, Howard, you're not Alan fucking Sugar…

Pause.

No, I can't ask a friend.

Pause.

Her voice breaks.

Because I haven't *got* a friend.

Pause.

Thank you, bye. Phone Tess, will you?

SHEILA. I'd offer to be your friend but we've got nothing in common, have we?

SELINA. We've both got children. They're always with you, aren't they. Inside your head. Clamouring for attention. Poor kids.

COURTNEY. Do you want to hold the baby?

SELINA. I'm no good with babies. I was hopeless with my own.

Pause.

They hate me for it now.

SHEILA. It couldn't have been that bad for them. You're on good money, you've got two houses and we know you've got a tree house.

SHEILA *and* KERRY *laugh.*

SELINA. Oh, that fucking tree house! It'll be on my grave-stone, 'Here lies Selina Snow. She bought a tree house with her Parliamentary expenses…

Getting upset.

…so that her poor neglected children would have something to play in while their mother was at work, telling lies for Peter Mandelson!' I shouldn't have bothered, they never play in the bloody thing. I was reprimanded at conference. A delegate with terrible teeth believed that I was a disgrace to the memory of the Jarrow marchers. He got a standing ovation. Gordon clapped until his hands were raw.

COURTNEY. Mam, can McKenzie have ballet lessons when she's older?

KERRY. It's highly unlikely. She's not going to grow any bigger, is she?

COURTNEY *ignores* KERRY.

Is she, Courtney?

SELINA. Who's the baby's father?

There is a very awkward silence. VINCENT *stops skiing.*

SHEILA. We don't know.

COURTNEY. There were five of them.

COURTNEY *tries to divert* SELINA.

(*To* SELINA.) What are your children called?

SELINA. Will and Tess.

COURTNEY. Which one do you like the best?

SELINA. Tess. She's a bit of a diva but at least she's speaking to me, Will doesn't speak. He sends me poisonous texts claiming that he got more affection from his Buzz Lightyear than he did from me.

(*To* COURTNEY.) You had five lovers?

COURTNEY (*upset*). Not lovers. They didn't love me. They didn't know me. I were just a girl walking home from school.

VINCENT (*angrily*). I'll kill them, Mam. I will, I'll kill them.

SHEILA. You won't get the chance, Vincent, because you can't go out, can you?

COURTNEY. If they catch you, they'll send you back.

VINCENT *puts his hands over his ears.*

VINCENT (*distressed*). I can't go back. If they send me back there I'll kill myself. I know how to do it so it's fast. You put your rifle in your mouth and pull the trigger. It makes a mess but they're used to cleaning it up.

KERRY *enters.*

KERRY (*shouting*). Vincent! Shut the fuck up! Get back on the Wii.

VINCENT *gets back on the Wii and is immediately in another world.*

SHEILA (*to* KERRY). Kerry, you'd make a good MP. You're opinionated, you get things done.

KERRY. You have to go to London, though, don't you? I couldn't go to London, could I?

SHEILA (*to* SELINA). Kerry took exams.

KERRY (*to* SHEILA). Mam, I took six and passed three. (*To* SELINA.) You can't do owt with three O-levels.

SHEILA (*to* SELINA). Kerry were the first in our family to get O-levels. We had a party for you, didn't we, Kerry?

KERRY. Turned into a street party, didn't it? It were a lovely warm night. We all brought chairs out and sat round in the road, drinking and laughing, all the little kids were running round in their pyjamas, it were a lovely night. I thought my life would change, but it didn't. Barry saw to that.

SELINA. Barry?

SHEILA. Kerry's first husband. He had anger-management problems.

KERRY. It weren't a problem to him. Just every bugger else.

SELINA. So things were alright then? You could go out then? So what changed?

SHEILA. The jobs went. The Leicester Road used to be lined with factories. Boots, shoes, socks, vests, pants, stockings, tights.

KERRY. When you walked home from town late at night, barefoot, carrying your stilettos, you knew you were nearly home because you could see the factories in the distance, they were lit up like a fairground, and as you passed by you could feel the machines vibrating under your feet, and if you stood stock-still you could hear them humming. In each factory there'd be somebody you knew on the night shift, a relative, a friend, or somebody you'd copped off with. I were never frightened to walk round at night then.

VINCENT. Did you used to get pissed up, Mam? Were you a pisshead?

KERRY (*suddenly angry*). Yeah, I did! And I'm proud of it! In them days we didn't shove stuff up our noses and fuck our brains up so bad we thought we was Nelson fucking Mandela, and that our back bedroom was Robben Island!

VINCENT *hangs his head.*

MARK (*into phone*). Right… right… yeah… (*To* KERRY.) What did you do with the suit?

KERRY. It's in the washing machine on gas mark three.

MARK (*into phone*). Too late, it's in the fucking washer!

A few beats.

(*Shouting into phone.*) Where the fuck am I meant to get fresh blood from?

KERRY. You could always slit your wrists.

MARK (*into phone*). I'll get back to you. (*To* SELINA.) They want you on the Six O'Clock but you've gotta be wearing your bloodstained suit and a bandage. Anybody altruistic enough to donate blood for the cause?

Nobody speaks. Everybody stares at MARK.

Okay. Twenty quid?

SELINA. Don't be ridiculous.

MARK. Okay. Twenty-five quid for an eggcup full. It won't be so ridiculous when you lose your fucking marginal seat. Pity is the only thing you've got going for you now, Selina.

He opens his wallet, takes out a wad of notes and shows it to the family.

Thirty. Think how much crap food you could buy for that. Yummy, yummy. Boxes of chicken dippers, Jammy Dodgers, mega-bags of crisps. Tin after tin of Spam. Blocks of lard: the spread of choice in Chavland. No? Alright, thirty-five. That would keep you in cakes for, let's see, a week!

SHEILA. You hate us, don't you, posh boy? You think we're animals and that scares you, don't it? You think we'll leave the estates and turn on you one day.

KERRY *plays at being a tiger. She growls and bares her teeth and claws.* MARK *flinches back.*

MARK. I'm going for a fag.

MARK *goes out.*

COURTNEY *goes on Facebook.*

SELINA. God, I'd love a fag. I haven't smoked since election night 1997.

SHEILA (*to* SELINA). How many re-counts were there, Mrs Snow? Was it four or five?

SELINA. It was four.

SHEILA. And how many votes did you win by, in the end?

SELINA. Three. It was the longest night of my life.

SHEILA. Three votes. That's me, Kerry and Vincent. Pity we can't go out.

COURTNEY. I don't know who I'd vote for.

KERRY. It's like choosing between three turds – they all stink.

KERRY *goes out to the kitchen.*

VINCENT. They're all crooks. They're just in it for what they can get. Did you know, Courtney, that a man bought a house for his ducks to live in? And that we had to pay for it?

COURTNEY. Well, that's not right, not when I'm sharing a bedroom with Mam.

SHEILA (*to* KERRY *in the kitchen*). You should vote, our Kerry, a racehorse died so you could go to a Scout hut and make your mark.

SELINA. The racehorse did not die! Emily Davison, the Suffragette, died! However, if she'd seen today's gormless young women with their crotch-high skirts and diamante nipples fighting in the street… she'd have stayed at home and embroidered an antimacassar.

The lights go out. The computer dies. The Wii screen goes black.

COURTNEY *screams*.

COURTNEY. Nana! I'm in the dark!

SHEILA. We're all in the bleedin' dark! It's only the leccy gone.

VINCENT. Where are you, Mam? I'm not 'aving this. No way. I don't like it. It were dark when Wayne had 'is legs and 'is arm blowed off. We was late gettin' back to camp. It were my fault, I 'ad the shits an' we kept 'avin' to stop… Don't let 'im come round here again, Nana, have you seen the way he looks at me… He's jealous of me legs. He wants my left arm.

SELINA. I'm sorry, Vincent. If I could wind back the clock…

SHEILA (*shouting*). Kerry! There's a new leccy card in my bag on the worktop.

SELINA. I like the dark. I could sleep for a hundred years.

COURTNEY. Waiting for a prince to wake you up?

SELINA. I've had my prince.

COURTNEY. Was he fit?

SHEILA. Good-looking.

SELINA. Not really. He left me in June 1997. He rode a white charger into the sunset with Clare Gibbons, a nail technician from Market Harborough.

KERRY (*off*). It's not on the worktop!

COURTNEY. How did they meet?

SELINA. He went in for a manicure. He was incredibly vain.

SHEILA (*singing*). 'You're so vain, I bet you think this song is about you.

SELINA *joins in*.

You're so vain, I bet you think this song is about you, don't you? Don't you?'

The lights go on. The electrical machines come back to life.

KERRY *enters. She is dressed in* SELINA'*s clean cream suit and her own white stilettos. She has done her hair and make-up.*

KERRY. I couldn't resist trying it on. It's still damp. But it feels lovely. The sun's shining outside. Spring's here.

She goes to window and opens the curtain. Sunshine floods in.

(*To* SELINA.) You feel like getting things done in a suit like this.

SELINA. Keep it on. Do something. Go somewhere.

COURTNEY. No, she can't. Mam! McKenzie's due for a bottle. I don't know how to… mix the stuff.

KERRY. Give it to me.

COURTNEY. Don't call her 'it'!

She passes the baby to KERRY.

KERRY. Vincent, tomorrow morning I'm ringing Colonel Hind and then me and Selina are gonna get you a medical discharge. Your head's not right, Vince. Courtney, would I ever harm a real baby?

COURTNEY. No.

KERRY *holds McKenzie by one leg and swings her around. The baby cries.*

Don't, Mam! You're hurting her!

SELINA. You'll pull her leg out of its socket!

SHEILA. Kerry, that's cruel! Enough! Tell her and get it done with.

KERRY. Right, first you tell her where McKenzie came from, tell her, Mam!

SHEILA. Toys 'R' Us. You lost your baby, sweetheart. Remember?

Long pause.

You're a hard cow, Kerry.

COURTNEY. I knew it weren't a real baby.

VINCENT. I knew it were me who put the batteries in.

KERRY. You can't shield us from the world, Mam.

SHEILA. It's not the world I knew, Kerry.

KERRY. It's the only one we've got, though, Mam.

MARK *comes in. He stares at* KERRY.

MARK. They're sending a car at five.

SELINA. I'm not going.

MARK. It's the Six O'Clock!

SELINA. I don't care, I'm not going. I'm sick of listening to the lies and obfuscations that drip out of my mendacious mouth.

MARK. And do you think the electorate want or can take the truth?

SELINA. Which is?

MARK. That nobody knows anything. Not the people at the top or the pond life at the bottom.

SELINA. It would be a novelty, though, wouldn't it? Admitting that there was no solution to the Middle East, or inequality, or why Noel Edmonds is back on television.

It would be fun finding out.

MARK. The Party machine will crush you into dust. You'll get no support...

KERRY. She will, she'll get mine.

MARK (*walking towards the door*). Support from a slapper!

He laughs and goes out.

COURTNEY (*shouting after him*). She can't be a slapper! She ain't thirty-five yet!

KERRY *pins the rosette on to her suit jacket.*

SHEILA. You going out then, Kerry?

KERRY. I am. I'm going canvassing.

SHEILA. Take care, duck.

VINCENT. You're brave, Mam... Braver than me.

COURTNEY. Don't go, Mam.

KERRY. I've got to. And so have you. You need to go to school, Courtney. You thought Russell Brand was a kettle.

SELINA. Thanks, Kerry.

KERRY. You got any leaflets?

SELINA. None I'm proud of. They're unreadable. Full of ridiculous non-words. But I've got a long list of New Labour achievements you could quote on the doorstep, what I'm most proud of is Sure Start...

SHEILA. Mrs Snow, the Sure Start mummies come in from the suburbs with their Ugg Boots and car alarms. The rag-arsed kids from this estate don't get a look-in...

VINCENT. Don't talk about you know what.

KERRY. Mention *what*, Vincent? Iraq?

VINCENT. Don't talk about it!

SHEILA. You could mention the minimum wage.

COURTNEY. You could say that hair extensions should be on the National Health.

The rest of the family laugh.

What? What? If I'm not wearing hair extensions, I feel crap.

KERRY. Right, well, I'm off. Places to go, people to see.

KERRY *walks toward the front door.*

KERRY *walks out. The front door slams.*

Everybody goes to the window to watch KERRY *as she re-enters the world.*

The End.